Preparing for the 2020 California MFT Law & Ethics Exam

Preparing for the 2020 California MFT Law & Ethics Exam

Benjamin E. Caldwell, PsyD

ISBN: 978-1-7348735-1-1

Ben Caldwell Labs
6222 Wilshire Blvd, Suite 200
Los Angeles, CA 90048

www.bencaldwelllabs.com

Ordering Information:

Discounts are available on quantity purchases by educators, corporations, associations, and others. For details, contact the publisher at the above listed address.

U.S. trade bookstores and wholesalers: Please contact Ben Caldwell Labs via email at support@bencaldwelllabs.com.

To you
You've got this
Pass

Contents

Acknowledgements

Deep and profound thanks to Marcia Castro-Rohrer, Emma Jaegle, and Jeff Liebert, my teammates here at Ben Caldwell Labs, without whom this book would not exist.

Thanks to all of those who used and provided feedback on earlier generations of this book. Your feedback found its way in here.

And finally, thanks to Angela, Layla, and Keira for their unwavering support and encouragement.

About the author

Benjamin E. Caldwell, PsyD serves as Education Director for Sim-plePractice Learning and as Adjunct Faculty for California State University Northridge in Los Angeles. His research papers have been published in the *Journal of Marital and Family Therapy*, *American Journal of Family Therapy*, *Journal of Divorce and Remarriage*, *Journal of Systemic Therapy*, and else-where. He regularly gives presentations around the country on legal and ethical issues impacting therapy work. Dr. Caldwell is a California Licensed Marriage and Family Therapist (#42723).

Other books by Benjamin Caldwell:

Basics of California Law for LMFTs, LPCCs, and LCSWs
Preparing for the California Clinical Social Work Law & Ethics Exam
Saving Psychotherapy
User's Guide to the 2015 AAMFT Code of Ethics (editor)

Disclaimers

Neither this book, nor *any* book or test preparation program, can guarantee success on the exam. While of course we do the best we can to assist, and believe that our guidance here can be a critical element in a successful study plan, your success on the test depends on your ability to learn and recall key information, and apply it in the test setting.

The information in this book is believed to be accurate at the time of printing. However, mistakes can happen, and legal and ethical standards can change quickly. It is the responsibility of each individual therapist to make sure they are remaining current with legal and ethical standards of practice.

Finally, while this book discusses legal and ethical requirements for the practice of family therapy, it is intended to be used exclusively in the study process for the California MFT Law and Ethics exam administered by the Board of Behavioral Sciences. **No part of this book should be construed as legal advice or as a substitute for consultation with a qualified attorney.** If you are in need of legal guidance, your professional liability insurer and your professional association may provide legal resources to you at no cost.

Introduction

First thing's first:
<u>You've got this.</u>

The California MFT Law and Ethics Exam is 75 questions over 90 minutes, and it is *absolutely* a test that you can pass. You've taken a graduate-level course in Law and Ethics that was probably pretty good, and probably not all that long ago. But even if it was a while back or a bit lacking in quality, you can catch up with the current standards fairly quickly.

As licensing exams go, this exam is pretty specific. Later, when it comes time to take the California MFT Clinical Exam, you'll need to know the theory and interventions involved in many different models of treatment, you'll need to know crisis intervention, and you'll need to know a wide variety of additional information on effective clinical care *in addition to* knowing the legal and ethical rules governing the profession. But **this first test is just about those legal and ethical rules.** In that way, it's actually a better test all around: It's shorter, it's more clearly geared to public safety, and on your side, it's easier to prepare for.

You've got this.

About this book

This book is meant solely to help you prepare for the California MFT Law and Ethics Exam. It aims to be as efficient as possible in providing the critical, current information you need to know to be successful on the test.

There are four main sources for this book:

1) The *AAMFT Code of Ethics*, available at aamft.org
2) The *CAMFT Code of Ethics*, available at camft.org*
3) *Basics of California Law for LMFTs, LPCCs, and LCSWs,* available at bencaldwelllabs.com and at amazon.com
4) California statutes and regulations, a summary of which is available at bbs.ca.gov (complete California law is available at leginfo.legislature.ca.gov)

In addition to those sources, a number of other articles and books were used in the development of this book, as reflected in the endnotes. This is similar to how the test itself is developed: Licensed MFTs use source material common in the field, and develop questions assessing an examinee's knowledge of 121 "knowledge statements" outlined in the Exam Plan the BBS uses for this test.

That Exam Plan is a public document available on the BBS web site. Because it so clearly specifies what kinds of knowledge are needed for the test, the exam plan was also key to the development of this book: **Next to each header in the study guide, you will see small numbers that start with the letter K. These numbers indicate the knowledge statements, in the BBS Exam Plan, that are addressed in that section of the book.** As

---

* You might rightly wonder – wait, two codes of ethics? Short answer: Yes. The BBS has said in public meetings that they use both codes as reference points when writing exam questions and investigating possible unprofessional conduct. Thankfully, the two largely overlap. It's unlikely that you'll see exam questions on areas where the correct answer would be different depending on which code you're looking at, though you may see questions on areas one code covers that the other does not, or where one code is more strict than the other (the correct answer would uphold the more strict standard).

you'll see, this book covers all 121 knowledge statements used in the development of the exam.

It is worth nothing that this book is not a substitute for a graduate-level Law and Ethics course, or for the textbooks used in such a course. By design, it does not explain *why* the rules governing our profession are the way that they are, nor does it aim to offer detail about how the rules can be changed. This book is not appropriate as a detailed desk reference to California law for clinical practice; for that I would recommend *Basics of California Law for LMFTs, LPCCs, and LCSWs.*

This book also isn't a substitute for a larger text on ethics, or for deep understanding of the ethics codes themselves. For more detailed texts on ethical issues for MFTs, I recommend the following:

- ***Issues and Ethics in the Helping Professions*** by G. Corey, M. S. Corey, & C. Corey (10th edition, Brooks/Cole, 2018)
- ***Ethics and Professional Issues in Couple and Family Therapy*** Edited by M. J. Murphy & L. Hecker (2nd edition, Routledge, 2016)

Using this book

There are lots of different ways to study for an exam like this, and while none of them are absolutely necessary for everyone, they all can be useful. Do what works best for you.

There are a handful of citations in the book, which refer to endnotes at the back. Those citations are used for direct quotes, longer explanations that are not critical to your understanding of material for the test, and sources other than the main sources for this book noted on the previous page.

About the Exam

Test basics

The California MFT Law and Ethics Exam is a 75-item, 90-minute test. Of those 75 items, only 50 count toward your score; the other 25 items are being tested for possible inclusion in future test cycles. Of course, you have no way of knowing which exam items are scored and which are these experimental items, so it is in your best interest to do the best you can on every item on the test. All questions are four-option, multiple choice questions where you are tasked with choosing the *best* response from the available options.

The test is administered via computer at testing centers around the state, and can be taken at some centers outside the state as well. You can see a complete list of test centers by going to home.pearsonvue.com/cabbs (Pearson VUE is an independent company the BBS contracts with for the administration of their exams) and selecting "Find a Test Center." No personal items are allowed into the test centers, and they have strict rules about the clothing that examinees can wear, in order to ensure the security of testing. Some test centers have lockers where you can store personal items during your test, but some do not.

You will be seated at a workstation where your exam has been preloaded into the computer, and you are likely to be offered a set of earplugs or noise-cancelling headphones to use during the test if you wish. (Some examinees find these very helpful for blocking out the sound of other computers in the room, while others simply find them uncomfortable.) The Pearson VUE testing centers administer a wide variety of tests for federal and state government agencies as well as private businesses, so it is likely that the other examinees in the testing room with you will be working on several different kinds of tests. Once you've had the opportunity to get settled in and familiarize yourself with the computer you will be using, you follow the on-screen instructions to begin your exam.

Content

Considered as a whole (but without considering experimental items), the test will break down into the following proportions:

Topic Area	% of scored items	# of scored items (out of 50)
Law	**40%**	**20**
Confidentiality, privilege, and consent	14%	7
Limits to confidentiality, including mandated reporting	16%	8
Legal standards for professional practice	10%	5
Ethics	**60%**	**30**
Professional competence and preventing harm	18%	9
Therapeutic relationship	27%	13-14
Business practices and policies	15%	7-8

The exam is not separated into these sections; you may get questions from various categories in any order. These are merely overall proportions. Still, they can be helpful to know. For example, knowing that ethical issues surrounding the therapeutic relationship make up more than a quarter of the test, you may place an emphasis in your studying on this area.

Scoring

Your score is based on the number of non-experimental items that you answered correctly, out of 50 total. Every item is worth one point – there is no weighting of items based on difficulty, complexity, topic, or any other factor. There is also no penalty for an incorrect response; it is counted as 0 points, just the same as if the item were left blank.

The passing score on the test will vary from one test cycle to the next. Some versions of the test will be more challenging than others, so the BBS conducts careful statistical analysis of each test -- and of every *item* on each test -- to make sure they set the passing score appropriately. While the BBS no longer publicly announces the passing score for current test cycles, they used to. During that time, the passing score was consistently *around* 35 out of 50 scored items (70%). To the best of my knowledge, there has never been a test cycle where the passing score was above 37 or below 33.

Strategy

There are many different test-taking strategies that can help you perform well on the exam. Of course, no test-taking strategy will substitute for having detailed knowledge of the material you're being tested on. But strategies can help maximize your score by helping with items you don't know the answer to, and strategies can help with time and anxiety management.

In general, I defer here to your knowledge of your own strengths and challenges. You probably already know how good of a test-taker you are, and you probably already know what strategies will work best for you. (If you don't, it may be worth it to you to try the practice exam here in a couple of different ways, to see what strategies help you the most.) Just like for studying, the only bad strategy for test-taking is one that doesn't work for you.

If you're already clear on the strategies that help you the most on exams, you can safely ignore the rest of this section. If you're interested, here are some strategies specific to this exam that may help you:

1, Take the easy ones first. You can go forward and backward on the test as much as you like. Remember that you have a time limit and that items are not weighted, so a good way to start the exam (and possibly build some confidence) is to go through the whole test, marking the responses you are sure of. Then you can go back and spend more time on those items that need more time to consider. You may find that in a very short time period, you already have half or more of the test completed – and that almost all of those answers are likely correct.

2, Use the process of elimination. Even when you aren't certain of the *right* response on a particular question, there is a good chance you will be able to identify one or more of the response choices as obviously *wrong*. Eliminating wrong options greatly increases your chance of getting the question right, even if you're not ultimately sure what the best answer would be. One way of eliminating wrong answers is to notice when a question is asking specifically for a *legal* response or specifically for an *ethical* one – that will allow you to eliminate any response choices that would fall into the other category.

The line between legal concerns and ethical concerns isn't as clear in real practice as it is on the test. The fact is, the phrase "in accordance with applicable law" or its equivalent is all over our codes of ethics, and the (legal) unprofessional conduct category known as "general unprofessional conduct" can make ethical violations into legal ones as well. But for the purposes of the test, the two are clearly distinguished – in ways that can help you succeed on the test, if you understand which issues fall into which category. The table on the next page addresses where several common concerns **generally** lie: Legal, ethical, or both. There may be exceptions within each.

3, Don't get stuck in a rabbit hole. You have 90 minutes to respond to 75 questions. That gives you a little more than 70 seconds per question. If you find yourself getting hung up on an especially difficult question, move on. Make a mental note (or, if you're using the blank paper provided at the test center, an actual note) of the question you're struggling with and any responses you have ruled out, and then go on to other questions you may be able to answer more quickly.

4, Stay confident. You'll encounter some weird questions on the test – either things that just don't make sense to you, or items that are strangely worded. You may even see bad grammar, spelling, and sentence structure. Don't panic. These kinds of items may be the non-scored, experimental items being tested for possible inclusion as scored items on future tests. This is precisely why they do that kind of experimentation: They need to weed out bad items. It's still worth it to answer them as best you can, but if you can't figure some items out, don't let that shake your confidence in your overall knowledge. If a question is confusing, consider it *a problem with the question,* not a problem with you.

5, Go ahead and guess. Because there is no penalty for an incorrect response, if there are items you are truly unsure about, it is in your best interest to go ahead and mark your best guess. **Use the last few minutes of your test to mark your best guess on all remaining items you haven't already answered.** The worst thing you can do is leave an item blank, since

Legal, ethical, or both?

Legal	Both	Ethical
Informed consent for telehealth	Minors' consent for therapy	Informed consent for therapy or research
Privilege	Confidentiality	
Scope of practice		Scope of competence
Client access to records; retaining records 7 years	Maintaining records	Storage and destruction of records
Professional titles	Truth in advertising	Testimonials
Telehealth regulations	Telehealth competence	
		Monitoring impacts of personal values, attitudes and beliefs
		Countertransference
Ownership of records	Client autonomy	
	Non-discrimination	Cultural competence
Fee disclosures	Fees for referrals	Bartering
Child, elder, & dependent adult abuse reporting		
Involuntary hospitalization	Crisis management	
Insurance parity		Advocacy with payors
		Termination and non-abandonment
Providing *Therapy Never Includes Sexual Behavior* brochure	Sexual relationships	Multiple relationships
	Monitoring self for impairment	Assisting impaired colleagues
Licensure requirements	Supervision	

See the important cautionary notes about this chart on the previous pages. In real life, the categories aren't as cleanly divided as they are here.

Also, a quick reminder: Stuff like this takes a long time to put together. **Please don't share this or other content from this guide online.** Doing so violates our copyright (there's some irony in breaking the law while preparing for a law and ethics test), and ultimately drives up prices for everyone. Thanks for being awesome and not doing that. ☺

that gives you a 0% chance of getting the point for it. Even if you're not able to eliminate *any* of the response choices from consideration, guessing at it gives you at least a 25% chance of getting it right.

Accommodations

Accommodations are available for examinees with recognized disabilities. If you need accommodations, you will need to arrange for a letter to be sent from your health care provider documenting your disability. Common accommodations include a quiet room for testing, or additional time to complete the exam. More information about the process of applying for accommodations, as well as the forms that must be completed, are at home.pearsonvue.com/Test-takers/Accommodations.aspx

It is Pearson VUE, and not the BBS, that determines accommodations for examinees with documented disabilities. As a separate process, the BBS will also allow additional testing time for those who do not speak English as their native language. There are strict requirements to qualify for this additional time, however. The form to apply for this additional time is at https://www.bbs.ca.gov/pdf/forms/esl_specaccom.pdf

If you are considering applying for exam accommodations, it's important to plan ahead. All requests for accommodation should be received at least 90 days prior to scheduling your exam. Actual processing time varies based on time of year, application volume, staffing, and other variables.

While many examinees with disabilities report that it is beneficial to receive accommodations, I have also sometimes observed those who do not have recognized disabilities trying to receive accommodations. You should note here that 1) test anxiety is not a recognized disability, and 2) unless you genuinely have a disability, including a history of benefiting from accommodations, you probably don't need accommodations. Remember that the majority of those who attempt this exam pass on their first try, and among those who don't, rarely does inadequate time come up as an issue.

Before the test

Weeks and months before

The material on which you will be tested is largely consistent with what you would have learned in graduate school, particularly what you learned in your Law and Ethics class. So a lot of your preparation will simply be re-familiarizing yourself with that material, and making sure you're caught up on any recent changes that have taken place in the legal and ethical rules governing our profession.

There are, of course, lots of ways to **study the material for the exam.** Do what you know works for you. The law and ethics exam does not contain trick questions, and there is no "secret" way to study. The only wrong way to study is a way that doesn't work for you. If you work well with flash cards, make them. If you're someone who does better with reading and rereading, well, hopefully this book is helpful! The point is, trust your instincts and experience when deciding how to study, and how much. Some will find that an hour a night is all they can handle, while others will want to take several-hour-long blocks of time to study. Similarly, some find it more useful to study with friends or colleagues who are also about to test, while others prefer to study on their own.

The most important thing to do several weeks before the test is to **schedule your exam.** Review the list of test centers on the Pearson VUE website and choose the one that is most convenient to you. While all of the test centers are designed to have ample parking and similar testing conditions, you might want to consult with others who have recently taken exams at locations close to you. They can prepare you for things like the friendliness (or lack thereof) of test center staff, which can make a big difference in your testing experience. Note that the center you choose to schedule might not be the one that is geographically closest to you; you might find there's one farther away that is easier to schedule on your preferred day and time, or in a neighborhood that you like to visit.

One thing you may find helpful once you have your test scheduled is to **clear your test day of other obligations.** Arrange to take the day off from work, and don't put any other appointments on your schedule. You will want to focus squarely on the test. And once it's over, you will not want to go back to work right away. If you pass, you'll want (and deserve!) a bit of celebration, and if you don't pass, you'll want some time to shake it off.

Another thing to address once your test is scheduled: **tell employers, supervisors, and loved ones about your upcoming test.** Part of this is simply pragmatic: They will need to know that you will be entirely unreachable, even in the event of an emergency, during the time you are taking the test. (Cell phones are, of course, not allowed in the testing room.) But part of it is also to shore up social support: It's good to go into a test knowing that a lot of people are cheering for you, and will be ready to celebrate with you once you pass.

The week before

Since you schedule your exam by phone or online, you may not be familiar with the specific location of the test center where you will take the exam. It can reduce anxiety on your test day if you actually **visit the test center** during the week before the test. Try to go to the center in advance around the same time of day that you'll be going for the actual test. This can help you get a feel for traffic, parking, and the like. Based on how long it takes you to get there, you can better plan your actual test day, making sure to give yourself ample time for unexpected delays.

The week before the test is also the time to **wrap up studying**. Hopefully by this time you're feeling confident and ready. If not, it's worth taking an honest look at *why* you're not feeling that way. Is it simple anxiety about the test, or is it a recognition that you don't know the material as well as you should? Anxiety can be managed through relaxation techniques, time with friends, and perhaps a visit to your own therapist. If there are parts of the material you are struggling with, you still have time to shore up your weak points before going in to the exam.

The wrap-up process does involve studying, of course, but **take care of yourself** during this time. There is indeed such thing as too much studying: if it is interfering with sleep, your ability to care for your clients, or your relationships with loved ones, you may find that simply adding on more study time this late in the process will do you more harm than good.

Part of taking care of yourself can be to **adopt a mantra**, or a brief statement you can use repetitively to center yourself and calm your nerves. (A mantra can be part of a larger spiritual or meditation practice, but doesn't have to be.) Here are a few you can choose from, or create one that is a good fit for you:

> *It's just a test. It doesn't define me as a person or as a therapist.*
> *I am ready.*
> *I've had good education, good supervision, and good preparation.*
> *I will be the same therapist after the test that I am before it.*
> *This is a milestone, just one checkpoint on a larger journey.*
> *I will pass.*
> *My friends and family will love me the same no matter what happens.*
> *I know the things I need to know.*

Occasionally, people find that they are really not ready for the test at this point, and may consider rescheduling it for a later date. That's fine, but before taking this step, consider whether it is truly about your readiness, or whether it simply is a reflection of anxiety creeping up on you. If it's anxiety, putting off the test may just mean you repeat the experience a few weeks later.

The day before

The day before the test, spend time reviewing what you know and making sure you have everything ready for the next day. You may want to prepare a checklist of things to do and things to bring to the test with you, such as a photo ID, paperwork confirming the test time and location, and the like. (Remember that most test centers will not allow you to bring personal items into the exam room. Some test centers have lockers you can use to store personal items during the test, but not all do.) Make sure you eat well and get a good night's sleep the night before the exam.

The day of the test

Different people have different ideas about whether it is helpful to do some last-minute studying on the actual day of the test. Again, do what works best for you. Some find that reviewing material one last time increases their confidence, as they recognize material, get practice questions right, and generally go into the test feeling good about how much they know. Others find that continuing to review at the last minute only increases their anxiety.

The most important thing you can do on the day of the test is to keep your anxiety in check. Have a normal, healthy breakfast. (Food and drinks are not allowed in the testing room, so don't go in on an empty stomach.) Get a pep talk from your partner or a close friend. If you've chosen a mantra, spend time repeating it to yourself.

Before you leave home or work for the test, make sure you have the documents you will need to get in: your photo ID and the confirmation from PSI that includes the date, time, and location of your test. Without these materials, you may not be allowed to take the exam.

After the test

Unless you have a disability accommodation that requires paper-and-pencil testing, or there is some unusual circumstance that has led the BBS to do a review cycle at the beginning of a new cycle of the exam, you will find out immediately whether you passed the exam.

If you pass, congratulations! You will not need to go through another test until you complete your 3,000 hours of supervised experience for licensure and are sitting for the Clinical Exam.

If you do *not* pass on your first try, but there is ample time left before your registration renewal, then failing is largely inconsequential. You can take the test again after a 90-day waiting period, and pass on that attempt. (If you start early, you could attempt the test three times before your renewal comes up.)

If there isn't time to attempt again before your renewal, you can still renew your registration; the requirement for renewal is that you have *attempted* the test at least once. But once you renew your registration, when you apply to retake the exam you will need to show proof that you have completed a 12-hour CE course in California Law & Ethics for MFTs.

The BBS will not allow anyone to register with a second associate number, or to sit for the MFT Clinical Exam, until they have passed the MFT Law and Ethics Exam.

Additional information

If you have additional questions about the exam process or requirements, the BBS has made a great deal of information about the exam process available on their web site, at bbs.ca.gov.

Hopefully this book will be a helpful guide to the information you will need to know for the exam. The more you can integrate the information here into your understanding of clinical work, the better off you will be. Deep knowledge of the information is, of course, likely to be the most important factor in whether you pass the test. But it isn't the only factor.

The BBS has been lukewarm toward test-prep companies, out of concern that the companies may suggest there is some "secret knowledge" behind the test when there is not. All of the information you need to know for the exam comes from common materials in the field, including the AAMFT and CAMFT codes of ethics (freely available online), state law and regulation (also freely available online), and the same Law and Ethics textbooks (like my *Basics of California Law* text) commonly used in MFT graduate courses in the state.

The new CAMFT ethics code

In December 2019, CAMFT updated its Code of Ethics for the first time in several years. They made dozens of changes in this key document, but most can be safely categorized as technical or clarifying changes.

A few, however, represent real and substantive changes in the expectations of marriage and family therapists. These include:

- **Additional protected classes in non-discrimination standard** (adding indigenous heritage, immigration status, and relationship status)
- There is new guidance on decision-making when entering into **non-professional relationships with former clients**, to ensure that such relationships will not be exploitive
- **An expanded definition of prohibited sexual contact** includes sexually explicit communication in the absence of a clinical purpose
- **Gifts** are addressed for the first time. Giving or receiving gifts is allowed, though the MFT should consider the clinical and cultural impacts before deciding to give or receive a gift.
- Relaxed language on **concurrent services** now guides MFTs to avoid providing duplicative services, rather than avoiding working with clients who have another active therapist unless there is a written agreement in place.
- **Soliciting other therapists' clients** is now allowed.
- **Soliciting testimonials** from current clients is now allowed, unless the client is "vulnerable to undue influence."
- **Bartering** is allowed in limited circumstances, with some additional requirements including a written agreement.
- **Requirement for advocacy with third-party payers is softened** – language here now simply requires MFTs to provide truthful information to third-party payors, and to assist clients *when appropriate.*

We've made updates throughout this book to conform with the new Code. The BBS reported early in 2020 that examinees would start seeing exam questions based on the new CAMFT Code of Ethics in July of 2020, and that the new code would then be the CAMFT code used used going forward. (Recall from earlier that the AAMFT code is also used as a reference during exam development.)

To study the new CAMFT code in more detail, you can download it for free at camft.org.

Here we go!

The next section is a summary of information likely to be included on the exam. The BBS uses 121 "knowledge statements" outlining what they believe you need to know in order to practice therapy within your legal and ethical boundaries. They've been organized here in such a way that should make them easier to study and retain. I've kept the descriptions as brief and simple as possible.

This study guide is divided into subsections that correspond with the knowledge categories on the exam plan:

- Law: Confidentiality, privilege, and consent
- Law: Limits to confidentiality, including mandated reporting
- Law: Legal standards for professional practice
- Ethics: Professional competence and preventing harm
- Ethics: Therapeutic relationship
- Ethics: Business practices and policies

You can see that these correspond with the categories used when considering how the test itself breaks down into different proportions. Given the number of questions about treatment you are likely to encounter, some additional time in that subsection may be warranted.

If you have questions about any of the explanations here, or want to dive deeper on any of the subjects covered in this book, you best first stop is the primary source material used in the development of this book.

You've got this.

Good luck!

Study Guide:
What You Need to Know

LAW

Confidentiality, Privilege, and Consent

Understanding confidentiality K1-2

Laws about confidentiality. Unless a specific exception to confidentiality applies, MFTs are legally required to keep the content of therapy confidential. This means that they do not share any information about clients, including even the existence of a therapeutic relationship, with outsiders.

Laws about disclosure. While confidentiality is the default state, a number of legal exceptions to confidentiality exist. In fact, there are more than 20 instances in state law where confidentiality can or must be broken, and information shared with outside persons or agencies.

Those instances where confidentiality *can* be broken are less relevant, as therapists will typically err on the side of confidentiality unless otherwise required by law. However, there may be instances where a therapist breaks confidentiality because the legally *can* do so and they believe it is in the best interest of the client to do so.

More commonly, though, the times when an MFT breaks confidentiality are limited to those times when the law requires it. These times can be generally broken down into five categories:

- Suspected child abuse
- Suspected elder or dependent adult abuse
- Danger to self or others

- Legal authorization, such as a court order or client release
- Other, less common instances where disclosure is required

The first four categories will be discussed in greater detail below. As an MFT, you need to be keenly aware of them. The fifth category – those less common instances where disclosure is required – includes an investigation by a board, commission, or administrative agency; a lawful request from an arbitrator or arbitration panel; a coroner's investigation of client's death; and a national security investigation. These instances rarely come up in therapy (if I were you, I wouldn't try to memorize those instances). In the event of a national security investigation, MFTs not only are required to turn over client records, but are legally prohibited from informing the client that they have done so.

Understanding privilege K3-6

Privilege refers to information that can be excluded from court proceedings. Normally, all communications between a therapist and their client are considered privileged communications, meaning that they cannot be used in court. Other examples of communication that is usually privileged include communication between spouses, and communication between an attorney and their client. Privilege is specifically a legal issue, outlined in California law.

This is particularly important in therapy. Clients need to be able to trust that information they have shared with their therapist about mental health symptoms or other emotional problems will not be used against them in court; if that risk exists, clients will understandably be less open with their therapists about struggles in the clients' lives.

Clients generally hold their own privilege. In other words, only the client can waive their own right to privileged communication in most instances. Even when the client is a minor, the client is usually considered the holder of their own privilege, although the minor may not be allowed to waive privilege on their own. A judge may block a minor (or an adult, for that matter) from waiving privilege if the judge believes that waiving privilege is not in the person's best interest. In any case, it is never up to the therapist to determine whether privilege should be waived. That is up to the client, the client's guardian, another court appointee, or a judge.

Release of privileged information. By definition, privileged information cannot be used in a court proceeding. Privileged information may only be released in court if the client has waived privilege, or if a judge has determined that privilege does not apply, based on one or more of the exceptions spelled out in state law (see "Exceptions to privilege" starting on the next page).

Responding to a subpoena or court order. If an MFT receives a subpoena (a legal document requesting that the therapist produce records, appear in court, or both), there are specific steps the MFT is commonly advised to take. These include:

1. **Contact an attorney as soon as possible.** The MFT will benefit from legal guidance throughout this process.
2. **Assess the subpoena for its source and validity.** A subpoena from a judge is a court order – the MFT must obey it. A subpoena from a private attorney is different, and may be fought if the client chooses. Occasionally, an attorney may advise you to object to the subpoena, if there is something wrong with the subpoena itself or how it was delivered.
3. **Contact the client to determine their wishes.** Often, the client will freely authorize the MFT to release the records or appear in court. Sometimes, the client will prefer that the MFT assert privilege on the client's behalf, arguing that the therapist's records or testimony should not be made part of the court proceeding.
4. Unless the client has specifically waived privilege or a judge has determined that privilege does not apply, **assert privilege.** This is generally considered the appropriate default position for a therapist to take in the absence of other guidance from the client or the court.

Of course, if the client does waive privilege, or if a court determines that privilege does not apply, you must comply with the subpoena.

Treatment of minors K7

Treatment of minors. In most cases, parents provide consent for the treatment of their child. Anyone under age 18 is a minor under state law, and parents can consent for treatment on their child's behalf. If a minor has two legal parents, then typically either parent can provide consent for therapy for the minor.

If the minor's parents are divorced, consent becomes more complicated. The MFT should request a copy of the custody order to determine which parent's consent is necessary for treatment of the minor. In joint custody, typically either parent can provide consent on their own. If one parent has sole custody, typically only that parent can provide consent for the minor's treatment. If that parent refuses or withdraws their consent, the MFT should not treat the minor.

Other caregivers may sometimes bring a minor in for therapy. Another relative who lives in the same home as the minor may provide consent for the minor's treatment if they sign a "Caregiver's Authorization Affidavit." The necessary language of this document is specified in state law.

Minors as young as 12 may be seen *without* parental consent if the minor is mature enough to participate intelligently in treatment. That determination is made by the therapist. In these cases, the therapist still must either make an effort to contact the child's parents, or document why they believe doing so would be harmful. Parents do not have a right to access records for their child if the child consented independently, and parents cannot be forced to pay for services provided to their child without the parents' consent.

Documentation K8-11

Documentation of services. Documentation of therapy is both a legal and ethical requirement. Neither state law nor professional ethical codes define the specific *content* that needs to be in treatment records, and there are a wide variety of formats for things like assessments and progress notes. However, all MFTs are legally required to keep records that are consistent with "sound clinical judgment, the standards of the profession, and the nature of the services being rendered" (CA BPC 4982(v)) As we will see, there are some specific things that legally must be documented when they occur, such as client releases of information and specific consent for tele-health services.

Maintenance and disposal of records. Under state law, records must be maintained for at least 7 years following the last professional contact. If you are working with a minor, records must be maintained for at least 7 years after the minor turns 18.

During the time you are maintaining records, of course you must take reasonable steps to ensure they are secure and confidential. When the time comes that you dispose of old client records, this disposal must also be done in a manner that protects security and confidentiality. An MFT should never simply throw old client files in the trash.

Client access to records. Clients generally have a legal right to access their records, though there are some limitations on this. Unless you believe that the release of records to the client would be harmful, you must comply with their request in a timely manner: Within 5 days if the client simply wants to inspect their records, and within 15 days if the client wants a copy of their record. You cannot refuse a client's request for records simply because they owe you money. You can, however, charge for reasonable costs associated with accessing and copying the client's file, and you can provide a summary of the file rather than the full record if you prefer (this typically must be within 10 days of the client's request). Any client who inspects their record and believes some part of it to be incomplete or incorrect can submit a brief statement to be included in the client file.

If you believe that releasing records to a client would be harmful to them, you may refuse to do so. If you refuse, you need to document the request and your reason for refusal. The client may then request that a third-party professional review the records to see whether that third party agrees with you that the record should not be released.

In the case of couple or family treatment, MFTs get consent from all members of the treatment unit prior to releasing records. This is an ethical requirement.

Release of records to others. Records of treatment can be released to third parties if the client requests it or if there is some other appropriate legal authorization. Most commonly, clients request that their records be forwarded to another therapist or health care provider for continuity of care, or they request that records be provided to their insurance company for the purpose of receiving reimbursement.

When a client requests that their records be released to a third party, this request typically must be in writing, and it must be signed and dated by the client or their legal representative.

There are some instances when a specific authorization to release information is *not* required by law, such as when the information is needed by another provider or health care facility to for the purposes of diagnosis or treatment (in an emergency, for example, there may not be time to gather written authorization), or when the information is required as part of a billing process.

Records are also sometimes released by court order, which is its own form of legal authorization. Subpoenas and court orders are discussed further in the section on Confidentiality & Privilege.

Telehealth laws K12-13

Telehealth consent. Under California law, therapists who offer services via telemedicine are legally required to first obtain specific consent for telemedicine (the consent can be verbal or in writing) and document this in the client's file. Failure to do so is considered unprofessional conduct. While simply scheduling sessions by phone or email would likely not qualify as telehealth, providing therapy by phone or videoconference certainly would. (Note that throughout this book, "telemedicine" and "telehealth" are used interchangeably.)

Telehealth delivery. California and federal laws govern the delivery of services by telehealth. When delivering services by telehealth, all of the laws regarding scope of practice, client confidentiality, and client rights to information and records continue to apply. MFTs must be particularly cautious when considering using telemedicine to treat clients located outside of California, as a California MFT license only governs services provided to clients who are physically located within the state at the time of service.

Under regulations adopted in 2016, California MFTs wishing to conduct therapy via telehealth need to take several specific steps. *At the start* of engaging a client in telehealth, the MFT must:

- Get specific telehealth consent (as noted above)
- Inform clients of the risks and limitations of telehealth services
- Provide the client with the MFT's licensure/registration information
- Document efforts to locate crisis resources local to the client

If that last one sounds a little stilted, that's because it is. A low-risk client wouldn't require the same effort to locate crisis resources local to them as a high-risk client would. So based on your assessment of client risk, you may locate crisis resources local to them just in case they're needed. Whatever you do in this area, it should be documented.

In addition to the steps above, the MFT must do the following *at each instance* of telehealth:

- Obtain and document the client's full name and current location (this should be an address, to confirm that you are qualified to provide services where they are)
- Assess whether the client is appropriate for telehealth (this may be based on their symptoms, and also may be based on the technology and privacy available to the client at that time)
- Use best practices for security and confidentiality

HIPAA. Under the Health Insurance Portability and Accountability Act (HIPAA), MFTs covered by the act have specific additional responsibilities to protect the privacy of client records. Among the requirements:

- Designating a privacy official
- Informing clients and staff of privacy policy and procedures
- Disciplining staff members who violate privacy or security rules
- Repairing harmful effects of privacy violations
- Maintaining safeguards against the release of private information
- Having complaint procedures for violations of privacy
- Ensuring confidentiality of electronic health information

- Protecting against threats to information security
- Notifying the department of Health and Human Services of breaches of unsecured health information
- Getting client permission before communicating via unsecured email

Obviously, memorizing that whole list would take a fair amount of brain space. It may work best to simply recall that under HIPAA, MFTs need to have and enforce specific policies to protect the security and confidentiality of health information, and that clients are to be informed of the relevant policies. Most MFTs covered under HIPAA provide clients with a Notice of Privacy Policies that outlines how private information is gathered and used.

There is a specific category of documentation that HIPAA calls "psychotherapy notes," which are a therapist's notes documenting or analyzing conversation with a client that happens in a private psychotherapy session. Within this definition, psychotherapy notes cannot include information like session start and stop times, diagnosis, progress, treatment plans, symptoms, interventions, or prognosis. Psychotherapy notes, as defined under HIPAA, must be kept separate from the rest of the client file and are not considered part of the client record. However, under state law, these records would still be subject to subpoena.

Sample Questions
See the next page for answers and rationales

1. A 14-year-old client consented to her own treatment at a nonprofit agency, which agreed to treat her for $5/session. The client tells the therapist (an MFT) that the client has been abusing a friend's prescription painkillers. Legally, the MFT should:

    a.   Notify the local child protective service agency.
    b.   Notify the client's parent or guardian, as the behavior is considered high-risk.
    c.   Work with the client to develop a plan to gradually reduce dosage and ultimately stop the client's drug use.
    d.   Document the discussion and refer the client to a physician.

2. An MFT receives a request from a former client for their complete therapy records. The client's treatment occurred four years ago. When the MFT locates the former client's file, the MFT finds that the file is disorganized, and consists mostly of brief, handwritten notes. The MFT, whose current record-keeping is much improved, is embarrassed by the state of this old file. How should the MFT address their legal responsibilities in this case?

    a.   Only agree to provide the client a written treatment summary in lieu of the full record.
    b.   Recreate the handwritten notes in a more structured, typed format, adding details as needed. Discard the handwritten notes and provide the updated record within 10 days of the client's request.
    c.   Refuse to release the file, on the grounds that it may be damaging to the MFT's relationship with the former client.
    d.   Release the file in its current form, and offer to address any questions the former client may have.

Sample Questions: Answers and Rationales

1. A 14-year-old client consented to her own treatment at a nonprofit agency, which agreed to treat her for $5/session. The client tells the therapist (an MFT) that the client has been abusing a friend's prescription painkillers. Legally, the MFT should:

    a. **Incorrect.** Notify the local child protective service agency.

    b. **Incorrect.** Notify the client's parent or guardian, as the behavior is considered high-risk.

    c. **Incorrect.** Work with the client to develop a plan to gradually reduce dosage and ultimately stop the client's drug use.

    d. **CORRECT.** Document the discussion and refer the client to a physician.

Drug use, in and of itself, is not considered child abuse (a). No such report is needed. Since the client consented to treatment on their own, the parents do not have a right to the client's records; even a high-risk behavior would not be disclosed (b) unless doing so was to prevent imminent danger. Advising the client on reducing prescription drug dosage would be considered giving medical advice and is out of an MFT's scope of practice. A referral to a physician (d) is appropriate.

2. An MFT receives a request from a former client for their complete therapy records. The client's treatment occurred four years ago. When the MFT locates the former client's file, the MFT finds that the file is disorganized, and consists mostly of brief, handwritten notes. The MFT, whose current record-keeping is much improved, is embarrassed by the state of this old file. How should the MFT address their legal responsibilities in this case?

a. **Incorrect.** Only agree to provide the client a written treatment summary in lieu of the full record.
b. **Incorrect.** Recreate the handwritten notes in a more structured, typed format, adding details as needed. Discard the handwritten notes and provide the updated record within 10 days of the client's request.
c. **Incorrect.** Refuse to release the file, on the grounds that it may be damaging to the MFT's relationship with the former client.
d. **CORRECT.** Release the file in its current form, and offer to address any questions the former client may have.

While treatment summaries (A) are often preferable responses to requests for client records, in this case the client specifically requested their *complete* record. With some limitations, they have a legal right to that record. Altering the record and presenting it as if it were the original record (B) could be considered fraud. While MFTs can refuse to release records if they believe doing so would harm the client, there's nothing in the question to suggest such risk of harm. The MFT's embarrassment is not adequate justification to refuse a record request (C). The MFT is obligated to release the file. Offering to address any questions is not a legal obligation, but may alleviate any confusion on the part of the client.

LAW
Limits of Confidentiality

| Scored exam questions (approximate): | 8 |

Exceptions to confidentiality: Child abuse K18-19

Laws about reporting child abuse. MFTs are **mandated reporters** of suspected child abuse when serving in our professional roles. In other words, we are required to report abuse we observe or suspect while in the office, but are not required to report abuse we observe or suspect at the grocery store, at home, or in other non-professional settings.

Your mandated reporting responsibilities are triggered when, in your professional role, you develop **reasonable suspicion** that a minor has been abused. Reasonable suspicion is a specific term with a specific meaning. As the law is written, if another MFT with similar training and experience, when presented with the same information, would reasonably suspect that abuse had taken place, then so should you. You do not need to be certain that the abuse happened in order to reasonably suspect it – for example, you do not need to have personally observed injuries to suspect physical abuse.

There are five types of abuse that must be reported, and one that operates on a permissive reporting standard. The kinds of abuse that *must* be reported are:

- **Physical abuse.** Anyone who willfully causes an injury to a child or engages in cruel or unusual corporal punishment is committing physical abuse.
- **Sexual abuse.** This category includes sexual assault, sexual exploitation, and what the law calls "lewd and lascivious acts." When minors engage in consensual vaginal intercourse, the therapist must consider their ages, using these two rules:

The 14ᵗʰ birthday rule:

If one partner is 14 years old or older, and the other is under 14, the therapist must report.

The drinking-and-driving rule:

If one partner is old enough to drink (i.e., at least 21), the other partner needs to be old enough to drive (i.e., at least 16). To put this another way, if one partner is *under* 16 and the other is 21 or older, the therapist must report.

For any other age combinations, the therapist should consider the age and maturational levels of the partners in assessing their capacity to consent and the nature of the relationship (i.e., is it exploitive or otherwise abusive) when deciding whether to report. When minors consensually engage in oral sex, anal sex, or object penetration, the current reporting standard is unclear. A state legal opinion applied the same age standards to these behaviors as exist for intercourse. However, the actual statute requires reporting any consensual oral sex, anal sex, or object penetration involving a minor, regardless of the age of the partner, even when the act is consensual. Given this difference between statute and legal opinion, questions about these behaviors are unlikely to appear on your licensing exam unless they clearly warrant a report. Of course, non-consensual oral sex, anal, object penetration, or intercourse will always be reportable when a minor is involved.

- **Willful harm or endangerment.** Any person causing a child "unjustifiable physical pain or mental suffering," or any caregiver who allows it to happen, is committing child abuse.
- **Neglect.** Even if it happens by accident, children are being neglected if their basic needs for adequate food, clothing, shelter, medical care, or supervision are not being met. A child does not need to have suffered actual harm for a report of neglect to be made. Note that a parent's informed medical choices, including choices to refuse medical treatment based on religious belief, are not neglect.

- **Abuse in out-of-home care.** This is given its own category for reporting purposes. It applies to kids who are physically injured or killed in child-care or school settings.

In addition to those types of abuse, **emotional abuse** operates on a *permissive* reporting standard, which means that you can report this if you choose to, but you are not required to. Children who witness domestic violence are sometimes reported as victims of emotional abuse.

Once you have developed reasonable suspicion, there are specific **timeframes for abuse reporting** that must be followed. You must make a report by phone to your local child protective agency immediately and follow up with a written report within 36 hours. This timeframe does not change for nights, weekends, or holidays.

Indicators of child abuse. Since the reasonable suspicion standard relies on MFTs having a shared understanding of the times when abuse should be reported, it is critical that MFTs are aware of common physical and behavioral indicators of abuse, neglect, and exploitation. The National Children's Advocacy Center has compiled the following lists of indicators. While none of these indicators by themselves would lead to a conclusion of abuse, they should lead an MFT to *consider* whether abuse or neglect may be taking place. Common physical indicators include:

- Unexplained bruises
- Unexplained burns
- Unexplained fractures or cuts
- Evidence of delayed or inappropriate treatment for injuries
- Multiple injuries in various stages of healing
- Injury or trauma to genital area
- Sexually transmitted disease
- Pain, swelling, itching, bruising, or bleeding in genital area
- Unattended medical needs
- Consistent hunger or poor hygiene
- Consistent lack of supervision

Notably, the law specifically states that the pregnancy of a minor, in and of itself, is not sufficient grounds to report suspected abuse. This remains true regardless of the age of the minor.

Common behavioral indicators of abuse and neglect include the following. As with all child and adolescent behaviors, a therapist must be especially cautious not to reach premature conclusions on the basis of behavioral indicators alone, as there are a number of potential causes for each of these that would *not* indicate abuse. However, these behaviors should get a therapist's attention:

- Sudden withdrawn behavior
- Self-destructive behavior
- Bizarre explanations for injuries
- Shying away from contact with familiar adults
- Sleep disturbances, including nightmares or flashbacks
- Substance use
- Anger and rage
- Aggressive, disruptive, or illegal behavior
- Frequent absence or tardiness from school or other activities
- Consistent fatigue or listlessness
- Stealing food
- Extreme need for affection
- Extreme loneliness

Exceptions to confidentiality:
Elder and dependent adult abuse K14-17

Laws about reporting elder and dependent adult abuse. Under California law, you must report any time you observe, suspect, or have knowledge of elder or dependent adult abuse. An elder is anyone age 65 or older who resides in California. A dependent adult is anyone age 18 to 64 who resides in California and has physical or mental limitations that restrict their ability to carry out normal activities or protect their own rights. Anyone admitted as an inpatient in a hospital or other 24-hour health care facility is, by definition, a dependent adult.

Reportable types of abuse include:

- **Physical abuse, which includes willful over- or under-medication.** Be careful with this, though – an elder reporting that they are in pain does not mean they are being abused. As long as they are being given the correct amount of medication prescribed by their doctor, it would simply call for a referral back to the client's physician to make any necessary adjustments in medication dosage or type. Various forms of sexual abuse are also included here as physical abuse.
- **Financial abuse.** This category is not a form of child abuse, but does apply to elders and dependent adults.
- **Abduction.** Specifically, the law refers to an elder or dependent adult being taken *outside of California*, or prevented from returning, against their will.
- **Isolation.** Elders who are physically restrained from seeing visitors, or who are being prevented from receiving mail, phone calls, or visitors (when the elder wants to see the visitor), are being isolated. In rare instances, a health condition may make limitations on mail and phone calls clinically appropriate, but there should be good medical documentation for such a decision, and other normal contact should not be restricted.
- **Abandonment.** Caretakers accept responsibility for the adults in their care. Abandonment occurs when a caretaker deserts their patient or gives up on their caretaking responsibilities when a reasonable person would not have done so.
- **Neglect, including self-neglect.** This is reportable not so that the elder or dependent adult will be punished, but so that they can be moved to a higher level of care if it is appropriate to do so.

Unlike child abuse laws, elder and dependent adult abuse reporting laws include permissive reporting of any other form of abuse not otherwise defined in the law. This gives an MFT broad latitude to report behaviors that the MFT considers to be abusive or exploitive, even if those behaviors do not fit neatly into any of the categories listed.

Similar to child abuse reporting, you do not need to have heard a direct report of abuse from the victim in order to develop suspicion that abuse has taken place. However, unlike child abuse reporting laws, the laws on reporting elder and dependent adult abuse say that **if you do hear of abuse directly from the victim, you *must* report it.** There is only a very narrow exception, for when the person has been diagnosed with dementia or another form of mental illness that would impact their memory, there is no other evidence of the abuse, *and* the therapist does not believe the abuse occurred.

The **timeframes for reporting** elder or dependent adult abuse changed considerably in 2013, becoming much more complex. If the abuse did *not* take place in a long-term care facility, then a phone report of the abuse must be made immediately to Adult Protective Services or another local agency authorized to receive adult abuse reports. You then must follow up with a written report within two working days. (If the abuse happened within a long-term care facility, the rules are much more complicated, sometimes requiring duplicate or triplicate reporting, and with varied reporting timeframes.) Recent state law allows for elder and dependent adult abuse reports to be made via Internet, in which case the Internet report should be done immediately, and it replaces both the phone *and* written reports.

Indicators of elder and dependent adult abuse. Common indicators of elder abuse include the following. As is the case with child abuse, it may be inappropriate to conclude that abuse has occurred based solely on an indicator here, as each of these can be caused by incidents that would not qualify as abuse. However, they can raise a therapist's suspicion, and suspicion is the standard for reporting:

- Physical or sexual abuse
  - Unexplained bruises, welts, or scars
  - Broken bones, sprains, dislocations
  - Restraint injuries (marks on wrists)
  - Unexplained bleeding or injury to genitals
  - Sexually transmitted disease
  - Medication over- or under-dosing relative to prescribed amounts
- Abandonment or neglect
  - Unusual weight loss
  - Poor nutrition or dehydration

- o Poor hygiene
- o Unsanitary or unsafe living environment
- o Inappropriate clothing (inadequate for cold weather)
- o Lack of needed medical aids, such as glasses
- Financial abuse
  - o Sudden changes in financial status
  - o Valuable items or cash missing from residence
  - o Unpaid bills when the person has money to pay them
  - o Unusual financial activity, or activity the person could not have done (e.g., large withdrawals, ATM withdrawal by hospital inpatient)
  - o Sudden appearance of unnecessary goods or services
  - o Signatures on checks do not match the person's
- Unusual caregiver behavior (can indicate risk of abuse of any type)
  - o Threatening, belittling, or controlling behavior
  - o Deserting
  - o Burnout (can be evidenced by mental health symptoms, substance use, poor resilience, irritability, or resentment toward the person being cared for, as examples)

It is important for MFTs to be aware that stress and burnout are common among caregivers, and these indicate a risk of abuse, but may also simply mean that the caregiver needs some time away from their responsibilities. Caregiving is difficult, particularly if the person being cared for has severe illness or dementia, is socially isolated, is physically aggressive, or has a history of domestic violence. These factors place the person at greater risk of abuse.

Exceptions to confidentiality: Danger to self or others K20-25

Identifying need for hospitalization. Under state law, an individual can be hospitalized against their will if they are a danger to others, are a danger to themselves, or are gravely disabled. In such instances, the person is taken to a hospital or other county-designated facility for assessment for up to 72 hours, which you may know as a "72-hour hold" or a "5150."

Legal requirements for initiating involuntary hospitalization. When an MFT believes hospitalization is necessary, having a client go voluntarily is usually preferable to the process of involuntary hospitalization. However, if the MFT believes the client has a mental disorder that is causing them to be a danger to themselves or others or is gravely disabled, and the client refuses voluntary treatment, the MFT can begin the process of involuntary hospitalization. In order for a client to be hospitalized against their will, a therapist must be able to cite specific facts (client words, appearance or behaviors) supporting the dangerousness of the client, and the conclusions the therapist drew from those facts. The therapist must then find what the county considers an "eligible professional" to actually write the 5150 application. (Usually a police officer or other person designated by the county serves this role. MFTs can be the eligible professional in some counties, but may need to first go through additional training and certification.) Ultimately, it is up to a professional at the facility designated by the county to receive involuntary holds to determine whether the client is to be involuntarily hospitalized. If that professional agrees, the client can be initially held for up to 72 hours.

Laws about confidentiality in situations of client danger to self or others. Danger to self or others is commonly understood as an exception to confidentiality under the law. The *Tarasoff v. California Board of Regents* case established that danger to a reasonably identifiable victim outweighs client confidentiality. An MFT dealing with a client who poses an imminent danger of serious bodily harm to reasonably identifiable victims must take reasonable steps to resolve the threat, which necessarily include breaking confidentiality. (See "Duty to protect law" below.) When a client is suicidal, the *Bellah v. Greenson* case established that therapists have a responsibility to act to protect the client's safety, and this can involve breaking confidentiality to have the client hospitalized if needed. If a client poses a general danger to others because of a mental health condition, *Tarasoff* does not apply but the therapist still can move to have the client involuntarily hospitalized if needed.

In each of these instances, the MFT breaks confidentiality. The MFT shares information about therapy with others who are involved in resolving the immediate danger. Even in these situations, though, the MFT should share *only* the information necessary to resolve the immediate threat. Sharing unrelated information about the client's therapy may still be seen as a violation of confidentiality rules.

If a *Tarasoff* situation arises where the therapist is able to resolve the immediate danger *without* notifying law enforcement, the MFT still must inform law enforcement of the threat within 24 hours. This relatively recent law was enacted to help law enforcement put potentially dangerous individuals into a database that would prevent them from buying guns.

Methods and criteria to identify when a client poses danger to self or others. Thankfully, there are good, brief ways of assessing clients who may pose a danger to themselves or someone else. Assessments for suicide and violence to others tend to focus on the following factors:

- **Ideation (thoughts).** Is the person actively thinking about harming themselves or someone else? For suicidality, are they romanticizing what their death would be like, for them or for others around them?
- **Planning.** Do they have a specific plan for how they would hurt themselves or someone else? Is it immediate?
- **Intent.** Does the person intend to commit violence? How sure are they? Some clients will fantasize about violence or death without any intent to ever act on these fantasies.
- **Access to means.** How easy would it be to carry out the plan? If they are considering suicide or homicide by gun, is there a gun in the house?
- **Past experience.** Have they attempted suicide or been violent with others before? How? Note that *previous suicide attempts* is the strongest risk factor for future attempts.
- **Protective factors.** What are the reasons the person has not hurt themselves or someone else so far? What would prevent them from suicide or violence in the future?

Demographic factors are also important to keep in mind, though these are not predictive of violence. While suicide is a leading cause of death among adolescents (because other causes of death are not common at this age), statistically, the highest risk for suicide is among the elderly (85+) and the middle-aged (45-64). Men are at higher risk than women. Whites and Native Americans have the highest suicide rates among various ethnic groups.

Duty to protect law. You are probably familiar with *Tarasoff v. California Board of Regents*, the court case that established a therapist's responsibility to act when a client poses an imminent danger of serious bodily harm to a reasonably identifiable victim or victims. In such instances, MFTs have a legal obligation known as "duty to protect." While this is not technically a duty to warn (and in rare instances, it might be inappropriate to warn the intended victim, such as times when doing so might trigger the victim to commit a violent act), the most common methods of protecting potential victims are to notify the victims and law enforcement of the threat. You also have additional protection from liability when you make reasonable efforts to notify both the victim and law enforcement.

The law does *not* require you to report or otherwise act on threats to property. However, threats to property are not considered privileged communication under the law (more on Privilege is below), which CAMFT has interpreted to mean that therapists may share such a threat with law enforcement, the property owners, or others as needed to prevent the danger.

Indicators of intent to harm. Obviously, the strongest indicator of a client's intent to harm someone is when they tell you directly that they intend to harm someone. However, this is not the only indicator a therapist should be aware of. Third-party reports of a client intending to harm another person may be treated similarly to direct reports, if the therapist believes that the third party is a trustworthy reporter. Threats made in writing or by other means may be considered evidence of intent to harm. Indirect statements such as "after today, she won't be around any more" may also be reasonable indicators, based on the MFT's knowledge of the client. Threatening behaviors may also qualify. Clients who are actively using drugs or alcohol may present heightened danger to potential victims.

Exceptions to privilege K26-31

Privilege refers to information that can be excluded from court proceedings. Normally, all communications between a therapist and their client are considered *privileged communications*, meaning that they cannot be used in court. However, there are a number of exceptions to this rule, including six that you may be specifically asked about on your exam:

1) The client makes their mental or emotional condition an issue in a lawsuit.
2) The client alleges breach of duty by the therapist.
3) Evaluation or therapy is taking place by court order.
4) A defendant in a criminal case requested the evaluation or therapy to determine their sanity.
5) The client is under age 16 and is the victim of a crime, and the therapist believes that disclosing that information is in the child's best interests.
6) The therapist was sought out for the purpose of committing a crime or avoiding detection after the fact.

Since each one of these exceptions gets its own Knowledge Statement in the Exam Plan, there is a strong likelihood you will be specifically asked to apply your knowledge of one or more of these.

Sample Questions
See the next page for answers and rationales

1. An elder client tells an MFT working in hospice care that the client was recently taken to a local religious gathering against her will by her 50-year-old daughter. The daughter is a member of the religious group. By the client's report, the daughter told her mother that "this might be good for you, being around people with good values" and did not bring the mother home when the mother said she was uncomfortable there. Furthermore, the daughter donated the cash in the client's purse to the religious group, despite the client's repeated statements to her daughter that the client did not support the group. How should the MFT respond to their legal obligations in this case?

    a. Report suspected elder abuse (specifically, kidnapping)
    b. Report suspected elder abuse (specifically, financial abuse)
    c. Report suspected elder abuse (specifically, emotional abuse)
    d. Report suspected elder abuse (specifically, isolation)

2. A 15-year-old girl is seeing an MFT individually for issues related to body image and self-esteem. Her parents provided consent for the therapy and pay for her sessions, but do not participate. The girl tells the MFT that she has been exploring her sexuality. While her parents were out of town, she had sexual intercourse with a friend's 19-year-old brother. A few days later, she had intercourse with another boy, an 18-year-old senior at her high school. The MFT should manage their legal responsibilities by:

    a. Reporting child abuse to the local child protective service agency
    b. Investigating to ensure that the sexual activity was not coerced or while under the influence of drugs or alcohol
    c. Notifying the parents of their daughter's high-risk sexual behavior
    d. Maintaining confidentiality

Sample Questions: Answers and Rationales

1. An elder client tells an MFT working in hospice care that the client was recently taken to a local religious gathering against her will by her 50-year-old daughter. The daughter is a member of the religious group. By the client's report, the daughter told her mother that "this might be good for you, being around people with good values" and did not bring the mother home when the mother said she was uncomfortable there. Furthermore, the daughter donated the cash in the client's purse to the religious group, despite the client's repeated statements to her daughter that the client did not support the group. How should the MFT respond to their legal obligations in this case?

    a. **Incorrect.** Report suspected elder abuse (specifically, kidnapping)
    b. **CORRECT.** Report suspected elder abuse (specifically, financial abuse)
    c. **Incorrect.** Report suspected elder abuse (specifically, emotional abuse)
    d. **Incorrect.** Report suspected elder abuse (specifically, isolation)

All four options share reporting, so it is safe to presume that reporting is a requirement here. The differences relate to the *type* of abuse being reported. The law surrounding kidnapping (a) requires that the elder have been taken across state lines, which is not stated in the question. Emotional abuse (c) is not a specific category of elder abuse in statute, though the elder abuse rules do provide wide latitude for therapists to report anything they find to be abusive to an elder. Isolation (d) is perhaps most clearly not appropriate here, as the daughter took the client to a social event. Financial abuse (b) is most appropriate here, given that the client states her daughter took her money against her will and spent it on a cause she would not have supported on her own.

2. A 15-year-old girl is seeing an MFT individually for issues related to body image and self-esteem. Her parents provided consent for the therapy and pay for her sessions, but do not participate. The girl tells the MFT that she has been exploring her sexuality. While her parents were out of town, she had sexual intercourse with a friend's 19-year-old brother. A few days later, she had intercourse with another boy, an 18-year-old senior at her high school. The MFT should manage their legal responsibilities by:

    a. **Incorrect.** Reporting child abuse to the local child protective service agency
    b. **Incorrect.** Investigating to ensure that the sexual activity was not coerced or while under the influence of drugs or alcohol
    c. **Incorrect.** Notifying the parents of their daughter's high-risk sexual behavior
    d. **CORRECT.** Maintaining confidentiality

The age combination of the partners, in both instances of sexual activity, does not require reporting (a). If either boy were 21 or over, or under 14, these combinations would be reportable. While it may be clinically relevant to explore the context of the sexual activity in more detail, the MFT is not obligated to do so, and in fact should not position themselves as an investigator (b). While the parents may be able to access their daughter's treatment records, the MFT does not have a responsibility to proactively inform them of sexual behavior; further, there is nothing in the question that would necessarily classify this girl's behavior as "high-risk" (c). In the absence of a legal requirement or allowance for disclosure, the MFT is legally obligated to maintain confidentiality.

LAW

Standards for Professional Practice

Scored exam questions (approximate): 5

Sexual relationships K32-33

Sexual relationship between therapist and client. Sexual behavior between therapist and client is specifically prohibited under California law. (Such contact is also specifically prohibited by both the CAMFT and AAMFT codes of ethics, which we will discuss in the Ethics section.) "Behavior" here is a broader term than intercourse.

Intimacy between therapist and *former* client. For former clients, state law prohibits sexual behavior for two years after the last professional contact. Sexual relationships with former clients after this time may still be problematic, and are further discouraged in our ethics codes. But they are not legally prohibited so long as two years have gone by since the last professional contact.

The *Therapy Never Includes Sexual Behavior* brochure. If your client informs you that they have had a sexual relationship with another therapist, you are required by law to provide for them the state-authored brochure *Therapy Never Includes Sexual Behavior.* Failure to provide the brochure is considered unprofessional conduct. Many therapists keep a copy or two of the brochure readily available in their offices; it also can be downloaded and printed when you need it.

Scope of practice K34

Your scope of practice is set in state law. It specifies what someone with an MFT license can legally do. Now, California's MFT scope of practice language (California BPC 4980.02) is long and a bit obtuse. So rather than quote the whole thing, we'll just talk *about* it.

The MFT scope of practice allows us to work with individuals, couples, families, and groups. (Throughout this book, when you see the word "client," it may refer to an individual, couple, or family.) The MFT scope of practice specifically allows us to use "applied psychotherapeutic techniques," making us psychotherapists. And it allows us to use the training we received in our required coursework – which is key to understanding that MFTs can independently diagnose mental illness.

MFTs can use psychological tests in our work, under two conditions: It has to be with clients we're seeing for therapy, and we have to have adequate training in administering the test.

One of the most important pieces in understanding scope of practice is understanding its limits. MFTs *cannot* provide legal advice, medical advice, or other forms of guidance that are outside the MFT scope of practice. Recommending that a client take a certain medication, for example, would be outside of the MFT scope of practice.

It also is helpful to understand the difference between scope of practice – which is set in state law, and is the same for every MFT in the state – and scope of *competence*, which is based on your specific education, training, and experience. Scope of competence varies by individual MFT, and is primarily an ethical issue. It is discussed later, in the Treatment section.

Unprofessional conduct laws K35

When a therapist violates professional standards, they are said to have committed unprofessional conduct. The BBS exists to protect the public, not the professionals, and will investigate and (if appropriate) punish unprofessional conduct when it is reported.

State law currently defines 28 specific categories of unprofessional conduct. For our purposes, it's most important to know what unprofessional conduct *means*: It refers to **actions taken in a professional role that are**

below minimum professional standards. Unlike criminal cases (where you could go to jail) or civil cases (where you might have to pay damages to someone you have wronged), unprofessional conduct rules apply to your professional role. Unprofessional conduct can result in action being taken against your license or registration.

The types of conduct defined in state law as unprofessional conduct include the following. The language here is lightly edited from state law, and grouped into categories:

Sexual misconduct
Sexual contact with a client or former client
Committing a sex crime with a minor
Committing a sex crime
Sexual misconduct
Failure to provide *Therapy Never Includes Sexual Behavior*

Scope of practice and competence
Performing or offering services outside of scope

Impairment
Impairment due to mental or physical illness or drug dependence
Drug dependence or use with a client while providing services

Confidentiality
Failure to maintain confidentiality

Crimes and bad acts
Conviction of a crime
Committing a dishonest, corrupt, or fraudulent act
Discipline by another board or by another state

Fraud
Getting or attempting to get a license by fraud
Misrepresenting your license or qualifications
Impersonating a licensee
Aiding someone else's unlicensed activity

Testing
Violating exam security or integrity

Supervision
>Improper supervision of a trainee or associate
>Violations during or involving required hours of experience

Fees and advertising
>Failure to disclose fees in advance
>False, misleading, deceptive, or improper advertising
>Paying, accepting, or soliciting a fee for referrals

Record-keeping
>Failure to keep records consistent with sound clinical judgment
>Failure to comply with client requests for access to records

Telemedicine
>Violating state telehealth standards

General misconduct
>General unprofessional conduct
>Gross negligence or incompetence
>Intentionally or recklessly causing physical or emotional harm

The category simply called "general unprofessional conduct" allows the BBS to act against you if you violate other law, professional ethical codes, or the professional standard of care while in your professional role. In this way, behaviors that are unethical can also be considered illegal, even if they aren't specifically designated as such in the law.

Now, **you don't need to memorize the entire list above.** Most of it, again, is simply what you would expect (and what is covered in this book). Knowing all of the categories will not be nearly as helpful to you as being able to determine whether a particular behavior qualifies as unprofessional conduct under the law.

When a therapist engages in unprofessional conduct, the client may submit a complaint to the BBS. The BBS then has an investigations unit that assesses the complaint, determines whether it is actionable, and investigates if appropriate. During this time, the MFT has the opportunity to defend themselves. If the MFT is found to have committed unprofessional conduct, the BBS can levy fines, place the MFT on suspension or probation, restrict their practice, and in severe cases, revoke the MFT's license (or registration, in cases involving MFT associates). They also may require other actions, such as regular drug testing, while the MFT is on probation or in order to resolve the disciplinary issue. The disciplinary process is meaningfully different from a criminal trial or a civil lawsuit; the BBS only needs to find *clear and convincing evidence* that a violation occurred to issue a penalty.

Disclosing fees K36

Disclosing fees. Under state law, you must inform clients before treatment begins of (1) the fee they will be charged and (2) the basis upon which that fee was computed. If you're confused about that second part, think about the sliding-fee scales used at many training clinics: *Client income* is the basis on which the fee is computed. As another example, some MFTs charge more for couple and family sessions than they do for individual sessions. That's fine, but clients need to know about this before treatment starts. Failure to disclose fees and their basis prior to starting treatment is considered unprofessional conduct.

Third-party reimbursement K37-38

Third-party reimbursement rules. Health insurance coverage has expanded significantly since the passage of the Affordable Care Act. Of course, insurance is not the only form of third-party payment; employers, courts, nonprofit organizations, family members, and others may be the ones who are actually paying for client care. MFTs need to be aware of the rules surrounding third-party payment, including the limits on information that can be shared with third-party payers.

Some of the key legal rules regarding third-party payment include:

- **Freedom of choice.** Insurance companies typically must reimburse MFTs alongside other mental health providers. Associates do not have to be reimbursed, though some plans will pay for services provided by associates.
- **Mental disorder only.** Most insurers will only reimburse when there is a diagnosed mental disorder. Some will cover services

like couple therapy when there is no diagnosis, but plans are not legally required to do so.

- **Protests and complaints.** Providers can (and generally should) appeal denials of reimbursement. Consumers and providers both can complain to the state about insurance company practices. Depending on the plan, it may be governed by the state Department of Insurance or the Department of Managed Health Care.

One of the most important legal rules regarding third-party reimbursement is the legal prohibition against insurance fraud, which can draw criminal and civil penalties in addition to action against your license. Any falsification of diagnosis, procedure code, amount paid, or any other information for the purpose of receiving insurance payment is insurance fraud.

Parity laws. State and federal law require parity in insurance coverage for mental health. What this means is that insurers cannot use a different deductible or other forms of treatment limitations for mental health that they do not apply to other medical coverage. Co-payments, deductibles, and treatment limitations (like caps on the number of visits or days of coverage) for mental health must be equal to or better than the limits placed on other medical coverage.

Advertising laws K39

Advertising laws. Essentially any public statement where you suggest that you offer therapy or counseling services to the public would be considered an advertisement – the law is purposefully broad on that. The only exception is church bulletins.

State law is highly specific on the **licensure status** disclosures that need to be included in *any* advertisement of an MFT's services. A licensed MFT needs to include their name, their license number, and their title ("licensed marriage and family therapist") or an acceptable abbreviation ("LMFT" or "MFT"). An associate needs to include their name, their registration number, their employer's name, an indication that they are under licensed supervision, and their title ("registered associate marriage and family therapist"). That title can be abbreviated "Registered Associate MFT," but the abbreviation "AMFT" can only be used in an ad if the ad *also* contains the fully-spelled-out title "registered associate marriage and family therapist."

MFTs and associates can advertise themselves as **psychotherapists** and say that they perform psychotherapy, as long as they clearly list their licensure type, something the law already requires anyway.

Therapists can advertise using **fictitious business names**, so long as those names are not misleading and clients are informed of the business owners' names and licensure status before treatment begins.

Ads making any kind of **scientific claims** must be backed by published, peer-reviewed research literature.

Any **fees** included in an advertisement must be exact; you cannot advertise fees in ways like "$95 and up." For this reason, many therapists and clinics choose not to list their fees in their advertising.

It is unprofessional conduct for any MFT to advertise in a manner that is **false, misleading, or deceptive**. Any claims that would be likely to create unjustified expectations of treatment success are also prohibited by law.

Payment for referrals K40

Therapists are legally prohibited from accepting any form of payment for referrals. (There is a parallel ethical prohibition.) This includes payment from clients as well as payments from the professional you referred the clients to (sometimes called "kickbacks"). The idea here is that referrals should be made *solely* on the basis of what is in the best interests of the client. If you are getting paid for referrals, there is at least the *appearance* of a conflict of interests, as you might make a referral based more on what will financially benefit you than on what will clinically benefit the client.

This issue has become more complex in recent years. In some communities, MFTs participate in "networking groups," which are organizations of professionals who sell a wide variety of goods and services. These professionals join the networking group for the specific purpose of referring potential customers to one another. However, because these groups often operate in a structure where members are rewarded for the referrals they generate (the reward might be the *absence* of a fee that they would otherwise have to pay to participate), MFTs in such groups risk being disciplined for violating the standards against receiving payment for referrals.

Sample Questions
See the next page for answers and rationales

1. An MFT with a new private practice is considering how to market their practice. He wants to operate on a sliding fee scale based on client income. How can he best fulfill his legal and ethical responsibilities?

    a. Develop a fee structure that is based on services provided, and not client income. Fee scales based on client income are prohibited in private practice settings.

    b. Advertise that services are offered "as low as" the lowest fee on his scale.

    c. Make no mention of fees in his advertising.

    d. Make his sliding fee scale a percentage of income, regardless of the income level.

2. The client of an MFT is on trial for fraud. The client is accused of submitting false claims to the client's insurance company, including claims for sessions that did not actually take place. At the client's request, the MFT had provided superbills and related documentation to the client to support her insurance claims, including those for sessions that did not happen. The MFT is called upon to testify under court order. How can the MFT best address their legal responsibilities in this case?

    a. Refuse to share any information on the basis of therapist-client privilege

    b. Contact the client and determine how they wish to proceed

    c. Acknowledge that the overbilling occurred, but describe it as an administrative error rather than incriminating the client

    d. Provide specific and detailed testimony about the scheme

Sample Questions: Answers and Rationales

1. An MFT with a new private practice is considering how to market their practice. He wants to operate on a sliding fee scale based on client income. How can he best fulfill his legal and ethical responsibilities?

    a. **Incorrect.** Develop a fee structure that is based on services provided, and not client income. Fee scales based on client income are prohibited in private practice settings.

    b. **Incorrect.** Advertise that services are offered "as low as" the lowest fee on his scale.

    c. **CORRECT.** Make no mention of fees in his advertising.

    d. **Incorrect.** Make his sliding fee scale a percentage of income, regardless of the income level.

Sliding scales are allowed in private practice, making (A) incorrect. Note that some insurance carriers have terms in their contracts effectively prohibiting such scales, which makes the "cash-pay" distinction important. An "as low as" advertisement (B) is considered misleading in state law. And a scale that is a percentage of income *regardless of income level* (D) would likely be considered exploitive of high-income clients, considering the high fees that could result. Option C is the best answer here; while MFTs are allowed to state fees in their advertising, they are not required to do so. Since each other option is clearly incorrect, this approach – removing fees from advertising – is the best one of the choices available.

2. The client of an MFT is on trial for fraud. The client is accused of submitting false claims to the client's insurance company, including claims for sessions that did not actually take place. At the client's request, the MFT had provided superbills and related documentation to the client to support her insurance claims, including those for sessions that did not happen. The MFT is called upon to testify under court order. How can the MFT best address their legal responsibilities in this case?

    a. **Incorrect.** Refuse to share any information on the basis of therapist-client privilege

    b. **Incorrect.** Contact the client and determine how they wish to proceed

    c. **Incorrect.** Acknowledge that the overbilling occurred, but describe it as an administrative error rather than incriminating the client

    d. **CORRECT.** Provide specific and detailed testimony about the scheme

Here, the client sought out the MFT to commit a crime -- that's clarified by "At the client's request." That is a specific exception to privilege (A), and one that we can safely assume has already been determined, based on the fact that the MFT is testifying under a court order. With such an order in place, the MFT is no longer in a position to defer to the client's wishes about testifying (B). The MFT has no obligation to lie on the client's behalf (C), and doing so would violate the general ethical principle of fidelity – in addition to being false testimony under oath, a legal violation otherwise known as perjury. At this point, the only available option to the MFT is to testify truthfully as to what happened. (You could, of course, entertain a side debate about whether the therapist should refuse to testify on the grounds of self-incrimination, otherwise known as pleading the Fifth Amendment. But that's not offered as an option here.)

ETHICS

Competence and Preventing Harm

Scored exam questions (approximate): 9

Scope of competence K41-45

Understanding scope of competence. Your scope of competence is defined by your education, training, and professional experience, and so your scope of competence is unique to you and can change over time. Scope of competence is primarily an *ethical* issue, though practicing outside of one's scope of competence is considered unprofessional conduct in state law.

Knowing your own limitations. Just as it is important to be able to identify actions that would be out of the MFT scope of practice, it is also critical to understand when issues come before you that are outside your scope of competence. You can't possibly have training and experience for every possible situation you will encounter in your practice, so acknowledging limitations in your scope of competence is not a weakness. It is good professional behavior.

Need for consultation. When a situation comes up in therapy that is outside of an MFT's scope of competence, a responsible MFT will consult with a supervisor or others to determine what appropriate next steps would be. In many cases, the therapist will work to expand their competence while continuing to work with the client.

Protecting client rights in consultation and collaboration. Of course, MFTs are encouraged to regularly consult with other professionals and community resources to promote quality client care. It is common for MFTs to collaborate and consult with physicians, teachers, social service providers, and other important persons in a client's life, on issues that are outside the MFT's scope of competence.

When doing such consultations, MFTs respect the confidentiality of their clients. Each member of the treatment unit must give their permission for clinical information to be shared with any outsider, unless an exception to confidentiality applies. Even when client permission or an exception to confidentiality is present, the MFT should only provide the information necessary for the consultation.

Expanding competence. If one's scope of competence is determined by education, training, and experience, then it makes sense that MFTs can expand into new areas of practice, or improve their competence in existing ones, by getting additional education, training, and experience.

Responsibility to remain current. The MFT field is constantly growing and changing, with new treatment models and new scientific developments occurring on a regular basis. The training and experience that make you competent to work with a certain problem today may be considered outdated and inaccurate 10 years from now. MFTs have an ethical responsibility to remain current with new developments in the profession, through the use of education, training, and supervised experience. This is part of the reason why licensed MFTs are required to get continuing education hours in each license renewal cycle.

Self-awareness K46-50

Impairments. Good therapists are keenly aware of their own limitations. If you are struggling with a serious emotional problem, mental or physical illness, or substance use, it can interfere with your ability to provide effective therapy. In addition, if you have a strong emotional reaction to a particular client – perhaps because their struggle mirrors one you have gone through, or because there is something in the client's behavior that you strongly dislike – you may not be able to provide effective services.

Responding to impairments. MFTs need to know the referrals and resources available in the event that the therapist is struggling with an impairment and needs to step away from client care, either temporarily or on a longer-term basis. (Knowledge of appropriate referrals and resources comes up multiple times in the BBS Exam Plan, as it is important in many different sets of circumstances. Obviously, the test will not ask what the closest hospital is, since the same test is being given across the state. But you may be asked about the *kinds* of client referrals and resources that would be most appropriate to a given situation. Referrals should always be appropriate to the level and type of client need.)

For the therapist, obviously seeking treatment is appropriate when the problem is a serious emotional problem, mental or physical illness, or substance use. If the issue is a strong reaction to the client, the MFT should seek supervision and consultation, and consider going to therapy. In whatever time it takes for the MFT to resolve their impairment, protecting the welfare of the client is the highest priority.

Methods to facilitate transfer. In some cases, the impairment of an MFT will lead to their needing to transfer clients to other therapists. If it is possible and appropriate, the MFT may have a termination session with the client, focused on transitioning them to a new provider. The MFT should provide appropriate referrals based on client need. The MFT and client should consider a Release of Information authorizing the transfer of client records to the new provider, and authorizing the old and new therapists to communicate to ensure continuity of care. The MFT should follow up with the new provider to transfer the records and coordinate care appropriately.

Personal values, attitudes, and beliefs. MFTs are ethically prohibited from influencing client decisions on preferred treatment or outcomes based on personal values, attitudes, and beliefs. (Going forward, I'll just say "attitudes" to refer collectively to "values, attitudes, and beliefs.") Obviously, it is important for MFTs to be aware of their own attitudes and how they might impact the therapy process. Therapists allowing for their attitudes to influence them might pathologize the behavior of clients the therapist doesn't like, leading to incorrect diagnoses and poor treatment decisions. They might show bias toward one or more family members, impacting the effectiveness of couple or family work. They might become overly friendly (or overly hostile) with a client. They might place their own belief about a particular problem above current scientific knowledge in the field. Ultimately, the therapist is likely to miss or misinterpret important clinical information, decreasing the likelihood of effective therapy.

Managing the impact of therapist attitudes. So what happens, then, when an MFT becomes aware that they have personal attitudes that are entering into the therapy room? It depends on the nature of what is arising. If the therapist is experiencing judgment or bias toward the client based on personal attitudes, the therapist should carefully consider how those attitudes are impacting treatment. The therapist may seek out supervision or consultation to ensure quality of care, and may go to their own therapy to identify the source of the attitude, working to change it if appropriate. If the therapist attitude is likely to continue interfering in the therapeutic relationship, the therapist may consider referring the client to another therapist – but must be cautious to avoid client abandonment, and to ensure that the referral is not discriminatory in nature. If the therapist refers clients out based on personal attitudes about race, gender, or other protected characteristics, the therapist may be engaging in discrimination.

Multiple Relationships K51-55

A multiple relationship (or "dual relationship" -- the terms are used here interchangeably) occurs any time an MFT has a relationship with a client that is separate from being their therapist. Not all multiple relationships are unethical or illegal, and some can't be avoided, especially in rural areas or in work with more tight-knit communities.

Problematic multiple relationships. Sexual or romantic relationships with a client are expressly prohibited, and discussed in greater detail below. There are some other kinds of multiple relationships that are also expressly prohibited. These include:

- Borrowing money from a client
- Hiring a client

- Joining with a client in a business venture
- Having a close personal relationship with a client

If in MFT engages in any of these same actions with a client's spouse, partner, or family member, this may also be unethical.

Not all multiple relationships can be avoided, especially if you are working in a rural area or with a highly-specific population. It is also true that not all multiple relationships are problematic. If a colleague tells you that you can't see a client because "that would be a dual relationship," they haven't adequately made their case.

Multiple relationships must be carefully examined to see whether they would **impair clinical judgment** or create **risk of client exploitation**. These two considerations are critical to determining whether a multiple relationship can be allowed. If you know and like someone in your community and they ask to see you in therapy, your liking of them would surely influence how you observe them clinically -- in other words, your pre-existing view of them would impair your clinical judgment. (Impairment can mean positive bias as well as negative.) Having a client who coaches your daughter's soccer team could create risk of exploitation, as you could use your knowledge of the client's personal secrets to push for more playing time for your daughter. The fact that you wouldn't actually do this does not eliminate the risk of it, nor does it take away your responsibility to protect clients from that risk.

Even when such risks exist, though, in some cases it may be appropriate to continue with the therapy. If you are the only provider in a rural area, for example, the best interests of the client might be better served by going ahead with therapy. You would then need to take specific actions to reduce the risk of impaired judgment or exploitation.

Managing boundaries. MFTs commonly take steps to ensure the integrity and boundaries of the therapy relationship. This can be especially important when it appears that a client is becoming confused about the nature of the relationship, or is wanting more of a personal or social relationship than what therapy allows.

Some examples of methods for managing boundaries include having a conversation with the client to remind them of the boundaries of therapy; maintaining a clear treatment plan with identified therapy goals; making sure all contact between client and therapist stays focused on therapeutic issues; starting and ending sessions on time; and, when clinically appropriate, limiting contact by phone or other means between scheduled session times.

Potential conflicts of interest. MFTs are ethically obligated to be aware of potential conflicts of interest as they arise. The CAMFT Code of Ethics specifically identifies providing multiple forms of treatment (individual, couple, family, or group) to the same person or family as a potential conflict. Another potential conflict emerges any time a therapist engages in a non-therapist role, such as consultation, coaching, or behavior analysis, with people who are or have been clients in therapy. In any instance of potential conflict of interests, MFTs have an obligation to clarify their roles, and to distinguish how any non-therapist role is different from therapy. In order to avoid any risk to clients, it may be preferable to refer out for additional services that are different from those for which the therapist was initially hired.

Potentially damaging relationships. Sexual relationships, which are discussed at greater length below, are the best example of a relationship that can be damaging to the client. However, they are not the only example. Other forms of multiple relationships can harm clients directly, through poor care or exploitation, or they may harm clients more indirectly, by reducing their overall confidence in therapy as an effective and worthwhile treatment. Social relationships between MFTs and clients can create confusion about the therapist's role, for example, and can hinder success in therapy by clouding the MFT's clinical judgment.

When multiple relationships can't be avoided. Some multiple relationships are unavoidable, and others don't need to be avoided. For example, some level of multiple relationship is created any time an MFT gets a new client through a referral from an existing client. Another example occurs in a rural area, where an MFT may have regular interaction with many clients at community gatherings. In these and similar situations, the CAMFT Code of Ethics requires MFTs to "take appropriate professional precautions […] to avoid exploitation or harm" (standard 4.2). In some cases, the precautions may be as simple as having a conversation with the client to reassure them of confidentiality and clearly separate roles. In other cases, more stringent precautions may be appropriate, like the MFT regularly consulting on the case with a colleague, or documenting their analysis of risks and benefits. The AAMFT Code requires that MFTs document the precautions they take when choosing to engage in a multiple relationship.

Sexual relationships K56-58

Risk of exploitation. The rules prohibiting sexual contact between therapists and their clients come from a fundamental understanding that because the therapist has power in the therapy relationship, because clients are often emotionally vulnerable, and because the therapy process happens behind closed doors, sexual relationships between therapists and clients are likely to be exploitive and ultimately harmful to clients.

This exploitation does not require sexual *intercourse*, and the legal and ethical standards around sexual relationships are worded in such a way as to include romantically intimate relationships and sexual behavior generally, even if there has not been intercourse. The CAMFT code even includes sexually explicit communication, when it happens without a clear clinical purpose. (If you're working with a couple on sexual issues, that might require candid conversation about their sexual behavior; that's obviously ok.) A therapist could not avoid discipline by simply telling the licensing board, "But we didn't have sex!"

Intimacy between therapist and client. As noted in the legal section, sexual conduct -- again, a purposefully broader term than intercourse -- between therapist and client is specifically prohibited under California law. Such contact is also specifically prohibited by both the CAMFT and AAMFT codes of ethics.

Intimacy between therapist and *former* client. For former clients, the CAMFT Code of Ethics reinforces state law in prohibiting sexual relationships for two years after therapy has ended. Even after that time, however, the CAMFT Code continues to discourage sexual relationships with former clients, due to the risk that they will be exploitive and harmful to the former client. The current AAMFT Code of Ethics includes a *lifetime* ban on sexual relationships with former clients.

Intimacy between therapist and client's spouse, partner, or family member. State laws about sexual relationships with clients and former clients apply only to the clients themselves. Under ethical guidelines, the prohibition is broader: Therapists *also* may not enter into sexually intimate relationships with clients' spouses or partners. The AAMFT Code of Ethics also prohibits sexual relationships with other known family members of the client's family system. The CAMFT code limits this to "immediate" family members, without further defining the term.

Therapy with former romantic partners. Just as it would be unethical to start having sex with a former client (subject to the rules noted above), it would also be unethical to accept a client in therapy who was a former sexual partner. This type of multiple relationship is expressly prohibited by the CAMFT Code of Ethics. Entering into a therapy relationship with the partner or immediate family member of someone with whom the therapist has had a prior sexual relationship is also prohibited.

While these situations are not directly addressed in the AAMFT code, it is likely that they would still be considered unethical under the existing rules on multiple relationships.

Sample Questions
See the next page for answers and rationales

1. In a rural community, an MFT is treating a client whose daughter is good friends with the MFT's children. Toward the end of a session, the client mentions that the client's daughter will be having a birthday party in a couple of weeks. The client says that they would love for the MFT's children to attend but they are nervous about the MFT coming. "I'm sure I'm just being silly," the client says, "but you know an awful lot about me, and it might be weird for my family to have you there." The MFT should:

    a. Address the client's projection onto their family, and consider it to be the client's discomfort, rather than their family's

    b. Offer to discuss the party at another time, as it would not be appropriate to do so during a therapy session

    c. Discuss the client's concern directly, describing the steps the MFT will take to protect the client's confidentiality

    d. Reassure the client that the MFT will not attend the party, and discuss the benefits and risks of having the MFT's children attend

2. An MFT occasionally encounters her first client of the morning on the subway, as they both live in the same neighborhood and take the same train to the MFT's office. One day the MFT and client see each other as they are both about to enter the subway station. The MFT realizes she left her wallet, which contains her subway card and cash, at home. The client notices this and offers to pay the MFT's fare. How should the MFT address her ethical responsibilities?

    a. Accept the client's offer, agreeing in exchange to reduce the client's fee that day by the amount of the subway fare.

    b. Consider whether the client would expect special treatment in return.

    c. Accept the client's offer, and once in session, draft a written agreement documenting the payment and the MFT's commitment to pay the client back.

    d. Accept the client's offer, verbally agreeing to pay the client's fare the following week.

Sample Questions: Answers and Rationales

1. In a rural community, an MFT is treating a client whose daughter is good friends with the MFT's children. Toward the end of a session, the client mentions that the client's daughter will be having a birthday party in a couple of weeks. The client says that they would love for the MFT's children to attend but they are nervous about the MFT coming. "I'm sure I'm just being silly," the client says, "but you know an awful lot about me, and it might be weird for my family to have you there." The MFT should:

    a. **Incorrect.** Address the client's projection onto their family, and consider it to be the client's discomfort, rather than their family's

    b. **Incorrect.** Offer to discuss the party at another time, as it would not be appropriate to do so during a therapy session

    c. **CORRECT.** Discuss the client's concern directly, describing the steps the MFT will take to protect the client's confidentiality

    d. **Incorrect.** Reassure the client that the MFT will not attend the party, and discuss the benefits and risks of having the MFT's children attend

This is fundamentally a question about maintaining boundaries in the presence of a dual relationship. Such relationships are common in rural areas (and in some communities within urban areas as well), and are not necessarily problematic. The MFT should actively address boundary concerns (C). Refusing to attend the party (D) may be more conspicuous and thus more problematic than attending it, considering the closeness of the children's friendship; perhaps more to the point, there's nothing here that demands such a reaction. Refusing to discuss the issue (B) places the boundary in the wrong place, suggesting that dual relationship and boundary concerns are somehow not appropriate for the client to bring up in therapy. Conceptualizing the client's concern (A) is a clinical determination, not a legal or ethical one.

2. An MFT occasionally encounters her first client of the morning on the subway, as they both live in the same neighborhood and take the same train to the MFT's office. One day the MFT and client see each other as they are both about to enter the subway station. The MFT realizes she left her wallet, which contains her subway card and cash, at home. The client notices this and offers to pay the MFT's fare. How should the MFT address her ethical responsibilities?

    a. **Incorrect.** Accept the client's offer, agreeing in exchange to reduce the client's fee that day by the amount of the subway fare.

    b. **CORRECT.** Consider whether the client would expect special treatment in return.

    c. **Incorrect.** Accept the client's offer, and once in session, draft a written agreement documenting the payment and the MFT's commitment to pay the client back.

    d. **Incorrect.** Accept the client's offer, verbally agreeing to pay the client's fare the following week.

Borrowing money from a client is specifically prohibited, ruling out (A), (C), and (D). Accepting a gift, however, is not prohibited. MFTs simply consider the clinical and cultural significance of the gift. Whether the client would expect special treatment in return is a reasonable question to consider regarding that clinical and cultural significance.

ETHICS
Therapeutic Relationship

Scored exam questions (approximate): 13-14

Informed Consent K59-64

Informed consent. In order for a client to offer consent that is truly *informed*, they need a reasonable amount of *information* about the treatment process. MFTs have an ethical responsibility to provide clients with appropriate information about the treatment process, so that the client can make an informed decision about whether they want to participate. Because treatment plans and methods can change during therapy, informed consent for treatment is best understood not as a single event but as an ongoing process in therapy.

Facilitating client decisions about treatment. Professional ethics codes require MFTs to provide enough information to clients that the clients can make meaningful choices about whether to start therapy. The nature of this information may vary by therapist and by treatment type. MFTs are specifically obligated to inform clients of the limits of confidentiality, the client's right to autonomy in decision-making (more on that below), and of potential risks and benefits of any new or experimental techniques. MFTs are also encouraged, but not required, to give clients information about the therapist's education, training, theoretical orientation, specialties, and any other information the MFT thinks will be helpful.

Client autonomy in treatment decisions. Clients have the fundamental right to choose for themselves what kinds of mental health treatment they will participate in. While there are exceptions to this, such as for clients who present an imminent danger to themselves or others and thus can be involuntarily hospitalized, generally speaking, clients can choose their treatment type, treatment provider, and treatment goals as they see fit.

(Some goals would be considered inappropriate for therapy, such as a parent bringing their child into therapy in hopes of changing the child's sexual orientation. While a parent is certainly free to pursue this goal, it would not be appropriate for a therapist to attempt to offer this treatment.) Consistent with this principle, clients can also discontinue treatment or change treatment provider at any time. Even when treatment is taking place by court order, clients typically are able to choose their provider. MFTs respect clients' rights to choose whether to start therapy and whether to leave it at any time. Of course we can and should discuss such decisions with clients, but we cannot require them to remain in therapy, or to remain in therapy with us, if they do not wish to do so.

Culturally and developmentally appropriate methods. MFTs should gain consent for treatment in a manner that is culturally and developmentally appropriate. If a client is illiterate, does not read English, or is otherwise unable to make sense of the informed consent document, their signature on it would not truly reflect informed consent. The informed consent process would be better served with a verbal discussion in language that the client can understand. MFTs also should be aware of the possibility that clients may be attending therapy against their wishes, at the demand of a family member; in such instances, it is important for the MFT to determine whether the client is truly providing voluntary consent for treatment.

Guardians and representatives. When clients are unable to make informed decisions on their own, their guardians and legal representatives have the right and responsibility to make choices on the client's behalf. Most commonly, this happens when a parent or legal guardian consents to the treatment of a minor. However, it can also apply when a client under conservatorship is put into treatment by their conservator, or when a court-appointed *guardian ad litem* seeks treatment for minors involved in a custody dispute. In these and other instances, guardians and legal representatives are responsible for making informed decisions about treatment that will be in the best interest of the client.

Clients who can't provide voluntary consent. When a client is unable to provide voluntary consent for treatment, the MFT remains responsible for protecting client welfare. Clients may be unable to voluntarily consent for treatment if they are under the influence of drugs or alcohol, if they have been involuntarily hospitalized as a danger to themselves or others, or if they are a child brought to treatment by their parents, as a few examples.

In these instances, the MFT would still take steps to promote client welfare and facilitate the client's ability to make decisions about treatment to the degree possible. In the case of a client under the influence of drugs or alcohol, the MFT may simply take steps to keep the client safe until the influence of the drug has worn off and the client can voluntarily consent to further treatment. A more thorough informed consent process may take place at that point. If a client has been involuntarily hospitalized, the MFT may remind them of their remaining rights. In the case of a minor, an MFT may utilize an assent agreement, which spells out the purpose, risks, and benefits of therapy in a way that is developmentally appropriate to the child, and allows them to ask questions about the therapy.

You may be wondering why mandated clients have not been part of the discussion here. Generally speaking, clients mandated to treatment by a court or other outside entity retain their right to choose their treatment provider and voluntarily consent to therapy. They may be required by a court to be in therapy, but typically, they don't have to be in therapy *with you*. MFTs working with mandated clients are ethically required to clarify the MFT's role and the limits of confidentiality that will apply to the mandated services. This clarification helps protect client rights, as they can choose whether to go forward in treatment under those rules.

Consultation and collaboration K65-66

Effects of concurrent treatment. When done well, concurrent treatment can maximize therapeutic gains. Coordinated care among multiple therapists can mean that family members receive individual therapy to work on their individual concerns at the same time they are receiving family therapy to address relational issues. This may speed improvement by addressing multiple levels of concern at once, and by reducing the homeostatic processes in family systems that can keep individual symptoms locked in place.

Concurrent treatment can also cause problems, however, especially when the multiple therapists involved are not in communication with one another. It is not in the best interests of clients to go to one therapist who encourages the client to create distance from the client's mother, and then to go to another therapist who is working to develop a closer relationship between mother and client.

Ethical guidelines for concurrent psychotherapy. The CAMFT Code of Ethics allows MFTs to work with clients who are simultaneously working with other mental health providers. Such an arrangement is not unusual if the therapists are working with different treatment units (such as an individual therapist and a couple therapist) or different problems (such as one therapist treating substance use while another addresses trauma). Under the CAMFT code, therapists discuss potential confusion or conflicts with the client, including whether consulting or coordinating care with the other therapist would be appropriate.

Working with multiple clients K67-72

Identifying the "client." MFTs are ethically obligated to clarify at the beginning of therapy which person or persons are considered clients, and the nature of the relationship the therapist will have with each person involved in treatment. There is a meaningful difference between a partner or family member *visiting* treatment, where they might offer input or moral support to a client's problem, and being *a part of* treatment, where they may be directly involved in therapeutic interventions.

When a couple, family, or group is considered the client, MFTs have an ethical responsibility to carefully balance the needs of the client with the needs of each individual who is part of the client unit.

Confidentiality. When working with couples or families, confidentiality becomes a key concern. If a client calls between sessions and informs the therapist of a secret, does the therapist have the right to bring that information up in a couple or family session? The AAMFT Code of Ethics takes a default position that MFTs maintain individual confidences unless given specific permission otherwise; the CAMFT code simply acknowledges that MFTs must respect the confidences of their clients, but also notes that the "client" may be more than one person, which brings "unique confidentiality responsibilities."

Most MFTs clarify at the beginning of therapy what the MFT's policy is regarding the holding of secrets. Some MFTs support a no-secrets policy, where individual confidences will not be upheld. Other MFTs prefer a lim-ited-secrets policy, believing this is better for accurate assessment of the couple or family. In either case, it is best for the MFT to have a clear, written policy that each individual participating in treatment has agreed to, and for the MFT to then stick to that policy.

In therapy groups, MFTs educate group members on the meaning and importance of confidentiality, and may ask group members to sign an agreement that they will respect the privacy of the group.

Preserving the therapeutic relationship. Of course, it would not be possible to list all of the factors that can influence the therapeutic relation-ship in family therapy. Nor is that necessary for an exam about legal and ethical practice. Lots of things can influence the relationship, not all of which are foreseeable. If the MFT keeps client welfare and the preservation of the therapeutic relationship paramount, the MFT will be able to manage most of these factors easily.

Consider two examples: In the first example, an MFT doing couple therapy begins to feel hostility from one of the partners, and is not sure why. The MFT asks the other partner whether it would be ok to meet alone with the hostile partner for a few minutes, and the other partner agrees. During this time, the hostile partner reveals that she is concerned the therapist is siding with her spouse over her. While this was not the MFT's intent, the MFT is able to change behavior moving forward, and offers and apology to the hostile partner.

In the second example, an MFT doing family therapy with a mother, father, and their two adolescent girls assesses that the girls' acting out be-havior appears to be related to conflict in the parental subsystem. The MFT discusses with the family the possibility of changing the treatment modality to focus on couple work. While the MFT reminds the family that he enjoys having them all come in, he believes the girls have done their job, and now it is time for him to do his in treating the family's core issue.

In each of these cases, the therapist took steps to support client wel-fare and the therapeutic relationship, when it would have easily been possible for therapy to go down an unproductive path. An MFT should be able to address therapeutic issues related to their role, the modality of treatment, and the involvement of outsiders openly with clients.

Potential conflicts. When an MFT is providing concurrent therapy to multiple people in the same family system – for example, when the MFT is seeing members of a couple both individually and as a couple – conflicts can quickly emerge. Individuals in the same couple or family may have competing and even incompatible needs. An individual may want to talk with the MFT privately about something they don't want their family to know. More practically, scheduling and costs can become difficult in these situations. MFTs are ethically obligated to carefully consider potential conflicts in these situations, and to take steps to avoid or minimize those conflicts. Good ways to do so include having a clearly identified "client," maintaining a clear policy on secrets, regularly addressing confidentiality issues, and following a clear treatment plan.

Treatment involving multiple systems or third parties. The AAMFT Code of Ethics encourage MFTs to routinely revisit discussions of confidentiality with clients. This is especially important when treatment involves multiple systems or third parties. In some cases, treating an adolescent systemically may mean involving their teacher, their religious leader, their social worker, and others in the therapy all at once. If these third parties start attending the family's therapy sessions, everyone involved should be clear about what the third parties' roles are in the treatment, and what information may be shared with them. Managing privacy and confidentiality in these situations can be a complex task. Of course, clients should give permission before third parties are brought in to treatment, and should be made aware that they can revoke this permission at any time.

Managing confidentiality K73-74

Ethical standards. Both CAMFT and AAMFT have standards for MFTs to specifically inform clients of the limits of confidentiality at the beginning of treatment. (Technically, AAMFT requires such disclosures, while CAMFT simply encourages them.) Of course, this is not the only time when it may be relevant to discuss confidentiality. The AAMFT code notes that therapy may require multiple discussions of confidentiality and its limits.

In addition, throughout the course of therapy there are multiple standards that relate to therapists' responsibility to keep information from therapy private. Consultations, recordkeeping, telemedicine, supervision, teaching/presentation, and preparation for moving or closing a practice are *all* to be done in ways that protect client confidentiality, unless a specific exception applies or the client has granted permission for their information to be shared.

Managing the impact of confidentiality issues. Particularly if an MFT has been required to share information from therapy, a discussion with the client about what information was shared, with whom, and why can help minimize negative impacts on the therapeutic relationship. Such a discussion can also serve to remind the client of the limits of confidentiality, and of the therapist's commitment to protecting the safety of any others involved. For example, if a report of suspected child abuse has been made, the MFT may want to discuss the role that an MFT plays in larger society in protecting vulnerable populations from suspected abuse. Ultimately, a conversation like this can refocus client and therapist on the therapeutic process and (hopefully) repair any harm done to the therapeutic relationship.

Managing crises K75-77

Assessing level of risk. When seeking to determine how much danger a client poses for potential violence, therapists tend to look most closely at a handful of issues:

- **History of violence or suicidality.** Previous suicide attempts are the strongest statistical predictor of a future attempt.
- **Plan.** Does the client have a plan for the harm they would inflict to themselves or others? Is it detailed and specific?
- **Means.** If the client is planning to engage in an act of violence, do they have the means to carry it out? Clients who consider gun violence who have guns in the home should be considered higher-risk than those who do not.

- **Intent.** Some clients indulge in violent fantasies to manage their anger or other feelings.
- **Imminence.** Is the client intending to commit the violent act as soon as they can? Obviously, the client with a more immediate plan is a more immediate risk. However, a client with a detailed plan that is more distant may still be considered dangerous, as any instance of heightened impulsivity (from alcohol intoxication, a manic episode, or any other reason) could lead them to advance their timeline.
- **Risk and protective factors.** Clients with strong social connections, a sense of purpose, and other protective factors are lower-risk than clients without these. And clients with meaningful risk factors, such as a history of violence or a recent significant loss, should be considered a higher potential danger.

The assessment of risk is a process that involves direct questioning of the client, observance of their behavior, gathering history and information on risk and protective factors, and also involving any other available information: Assessment results, information from the client's physician or others you have permission to consult, prior records (medical, mental health, court, or other), and anything else that may be useful.

There is no magic formula for determining risk, and recent research suggests that screening instruments intended to quantify client risk level aren't especially effective. When determining a client's risk level, consider the totality of their presentation, including their history. It would not be unusual to see a test question that presents one or two indicators of meaningful risk, where the most appropriate response is to assess further, so that you can more meaningfully determine the level of risk and intervene accordingly.

If you intervene in a way that involves the sharing of client information, you should be prepared to support this action by documenting specific client statements, behaviors, and risk factors that led you to the conclusion that it was necessary to do so.

Ethical obligations for protecting safety. There are no standards in the CAMFT or AAMFT codes of ethics that are specific to the protection of client safety. However, a number of standards are indirectly related. Both codes speak to an MFT's responsibility to advance client welfare, which would include protecting their safety. The AAMFT code makes specific reference to honoring the public trust. And the professions are fundamentally guided by ethical principles of beneficence (doing good), non-malfeasance (avoidance of harm), autonomy, fidelity (honesty and loyalty), and justice. Among these, beneficence, non-malfeasance, and justice all would suggest that an MFT has an ethical responsibility to protect the safety of both clients and the public.

Procedures for managing safety needs. As a general rule, safety needs should be addressed through the least intrusive means necessary to resolve the concern. You wouldn't hospitalize a mildly depressed patient, after all. Here are a few procedures for managing safety needs, ranging from the least to the most intrusive. This is not a complete list, and the options here are not mutually exclusive; it may be appropriate to develop a safety plan *and* increase the frequency of contact.

- **Continue to assess.** In the absence of any specific safety concerns, the therapist would simply continue assessing for safety in future interactions with the client.
- **More detailed assessment.** If a client suggests that their depression is deepening or that their hostility to others is increasing, but does not discuss any specific danger or threat, the therapist should assess the area of concern in more detail.
- **Development of a safety plan.** If a client has a history of safety issues, or is currently showing non-specific safety concerns (for example, a client with mild passive suicidality, but no plan or intent to harm themselves), a therapist may develop a safety plan. This plan lays out specific steps the client can take if their symptoms worsen. Steps usually follow a progression if early steps are unavailable or do not solve the problem. Steps may include contacting loved ones, contacting the therapist, contacting another on-duty therapist, and if these steps are unsuccessful, contacting a 24-hour crisis hotline or calling 911.
- **Increasing frequency of contact.** If you have been seeing a client weekly and you begin to have concerns about their safety, but those concerns do not rise to the level where more immediate in-

tervention is needed, you may ask to see them more often, or for the client to check in by phone more regularly.

- **Refer to a higher level of care.** Clients whose symptoms get worse or who become dangerous during outpatient psychotherapy may be better served through inpatient treatment.
- **Voluntary hospitalization.** Clients who pose an imminent danger to themselves or others and are willing to be assessed and treated voluntarily at a hospital will not be held there against their will. When a therapist is firm with a client that hospitalization is necessary, most clients will choose voluntary hospitalization over involuntary hospitalization.
- **Involuntary hospitalization.** If a client presents a major safety risk and is not willing to be hospitalized, an MFT may initiate the process of involuntary hospitalization. While most MFTs cannot invoke involuntary hospitalization, they can demand that a client be evaluated for a possible 72-hour hold.

Of course, if the safety concern is that the client poses an immediate danger of severe bodily harm to a reasonably identifiable victim, the appropriate procedure would be to notify the victim and law enforcement.

Best interests of the client K78-80

How legal and ethical obligations impact therapy. Our legal and ethical obligations exist primarily to protect the best interests of clients. They can have the side effect of protecting therapists, by setting clear standards of professional behavior (and thus protecting us from accusations of being unprofessional when we are not), but they fundamentally exist to protect clients *from* us.

Sometimes, our legal and ethical obligations can create an inconvenience for therapist and client alike. Clients may not read every word of a long informed consent document, and therapists may not want to spend time in therapy discussing the limits of confidentiality. However, failing to meet our obligations can place clients at risk in a variety of ways. We fulfill these obligations because it is good for clients, even when it isn't convenient.

Conflicts between legal and ethical obligations. There are many times when there is not a direct conflict between law and ethics, but they set different standards. For example, the law may offer a more strict standard than the ethics codes, or vice versa. In these instances, an MFT should follow the stricter standard, regardless of which set of rules it comes from.

For example, ethics codes require specific written permission from the client before recording sessions. The law is silent on this issue – getting written consent is *allowed*, but not *required*, under the law. In this case, the MFT is obligated to the stricter standard: the ethical requirement.

If there is a direct conflict between the code of ethics and the law – that is, if the law says that you *must* do one thing, while the code of ethics says that you *must* do something that is different from and incompatible with what the law requires – the law wins. MFTs should follow the law, and practice in accordance with the code of ethics to the greatest extent possible.

Conflicts between agency and ethical obligations. It is also common for MFTs to work in settings where ethics codes conflict with workplace policy. The AAMFT and CAMFT codes both require MFTs who face such conflicts to make their obligation to ethical standards known to the organization, and to take reasonable steps to resolve the issue in a way that allows the MFT to practice in keeping with their ethical responsibilities. The overriding principle is clear: Agency policy does not provide an excuse for MFTs to ignore their ethical duties.

Diversity and nondiscrimination K81-84

Ethical standards for non-discrimination. The CAMFT and AAMFT codes of ethics both prohibit discrimination in professional services based on the following factors:

- Race
- Age
- Gender
- Gender identity
- Religion
- National origin

- Sexual orientation
- Disability
- Socioeconomic status
- Marital or relationship status

The AAMFT code adds health status to this list; the CAMFT code adds ethnicity, indigenous heritage, immigration status, and gender expression.

While the AAMFT code simply says that MFTs "provide professional assistance to persons without discrimination" based on the factors above, the CAMFT code notes that MFTs do not "condone or engage in" discrimination, nor do we refuse services based on any of the above.

Diversity factors in therapy. Virtually any area of difference between client and therapist has the potential to impact the therapy process. While discussions of diversity in the US tend to center on issues of race, ethnicity, and (more recently) sexual orientation, a wide variety of other factors can impact a client's identity and cultural norms. In addition to all of the factors listed in the non-discrimination standards above, therapy can be impacted by differences between client and therapist in urban versus rural setting, educational level, regional identity, and many more.

Ethical standards for providing services to diverse groups. Therapists are ethically obligated to be mindful of all forms of historical and social prejudice, as this prejudice can lead to misdiagnosing clients or pathologizing culturally-accepted behavior. In addition, MFTs "actively strive to identify and understand the diverse backgrounds of their clients/patients by obtaining knowledge, gaining personal awareness, and developing sensitivity and skills pertinent to working with a diverse client/patient population" (CAMFT Code of Ethics principle 5.7).

Improving knowledge, skills, awareness, and sensitivity. So what can a therapist do when approached by a client who is different from the therapist in ways that impact the therapy process? While postmodern models of therapy encourage MFTs to allow clients to inform the therapist about the client's life and circumstances, it is likely to be inadequate for a therapist to take no other action to improve their knowledge and skills around the relevant diversity issues. The MFT could:

- Attend a continuing education training on working with the client's population
- Seek consultation or supervision from other therapists who identify as part of, or regularly work with, the client's population
- Seek out greater exposure to the client's population
- Read articles and other literature on the client's population
- Attend their own therapy to address issues of bias

Client autonomy K85-86

Collaborative relationship between client and therapist. It is the role of the MFT to *assist* clients in making important life decisions, not to make those decisions for the client. In fact, MFTs are ethically prohibited from making major decisions for their clients, such as decisions about entering or leaving a relationship. Instead we specifically inform clients that such decisions are up to them, and we respect their right to make those decisions as they see fit. In our role as MFTs, we help clients to understand the consequences of various decisions they may be considering, but the ultimate decision-making is up to the client.

This sometimes gets misunderstood as a ban on advice-giving. Many MFTs directly advise their clients, and this can be consistent with models of therapy that place the MFT in a directive, expert role. Even the assigning of homework, which is a common intervention in many therapeutic models, can be considered giving advice, and it is certainly ethically acceptable to suggest that clients try out specific new skills in the week ahead.

Methods to assist client decision-making. There are many ways an MFT can assist a client in decision-making without interfering with the client's autonomy in making those decisions. The therapist can help the client list various courses of action they could take in a difficult time, often expanding the possibilities beyond those the client may see on their own. The therapist can help the client foresee possible consequences of each of the possible courses of action, using current research as well as the therapist's knowledge of the client's specific context. The therapist can assess the client's readiness to act. The therapist can reflect and validate the client's excitement about some possibilities and anxiety about others. Each of these tasks facilitates the client making an important decision on their own, with the therapist's guidance and support.

Third-party reimbursement K87-88

Ethical standards for interacting with payors. Whenever you provide client information to a third-party payor, you need to make sure that the information you are providing is truthful and accurate, and as is the norm when sharing any confidential information, that you only provide the information necessary for that particular interaction.

Advocacy with third-party payers. Some clients are more able than others to navigate the complex bureaucracy of their insurance company. MFTs are encouraged, but not required, to advocate for their clients with payors when necessary and appropriate, so that the clients receive the care they need. MFTs can help clients in challenging denials of coverage or denials of payment, and may be able to assist clients in gathering needed information about their coverage or reimbursement processes.

One important piece of information is how able the client is to engage in such advocacy on their own. If clients can successfully advocate on their own behalf, there is no need for a therapist to inject themselves in unnecessarily.

Termination and referrals K89-94

Ethical considerations with interrupting or terminating. There are times when interrupting or terminating therapy is appropriate or necessary even when the goals of therapy have not been reached. You as the therapist may become seriously ill, or need to step away from your practice to care for loved ones. The client may suddenly be called to a military deployment or a new job out of state. The clinic where you are seeing the client may lose its funding. While we all hope these situations will not occur, the reality is that they often do, and an MFT is ethically required to be ready for such abrupt shifts. An MFT also must take appropriate steps when this kind of situation does happen.

MFTs are ethically required to have emergency procedures in place in the event that they become suddenly incapacitated or otherwise unavailable. These procedures may include emergency contact numbers where clients may reach the therapist or others able to take over client care. MFTs are also ethically required to be prepared for their own potential absence from (or inability to continue) care, which is typically addressed in private practice settings through what is called a *professional will*. This document lays out issues like who will take over client care in the event of the therapist's serious injury or death. The person assigned to take over client care must be given access to records so that they can contact clients to let them know of the change; for this reason, many MFTs include an authorization in their informed consent agreement letting clients know that a professional will exists and having clients agree that their records may be forwarded when necessary.

Having these plans in place minimizes the harm that may come to clients when a therapist is suddenly unavailable. However, treatment interruptions or sudden terminations are not always due to something happening to the therapist. Whenever treatment must be interrupted or terminated, regardless of whether it is because of something happening to the client, the therapist, the clinic, or the larger social context, MFTs have ethical responsibilities to *non-abandonment* and appropriate *continuity of care*. Non-abandonment simply means that clients in need of continued services cannot be left to fend for themselves; if treatment with the current MFT must be interrupted or ended, the MFT still has a responsibility to ensure that crisis needs are addressed and that the change in treatment does not result in harm. Continuity of care means that the client is able to receive continued care with another provider appropriate to their needs; most commonly, this means providing referrals that are local to the client, within their financial means, and able to treat the client's specific problem type and severity.

Knowledge of referrals/resources to provide continuity of care. In order to make those referrals when necessary, an MFT must be aware of local resources that can provide consistency of care to clients if therapy is suddenly stopped. Many MFTs maintain referral lists that include local hospitals and crisis resources, low-fee mental health clinics, psychiatrists, other providers whose services are similar to those of the MFT, and additional community resources.

Indicators of need to terminate. The clearest indication that it is time to terminate therapy is, of course, when it is clear that the client has reached their treatment goals, and no new goals have emerged. Even in the absence of having reached the goals of treatment, if a client regularly comes in appearing to no longer be in distress, and sessions are spent on ordinary social conversation, this can indicate that the client is ready to be done with therapy.

Client is not benefiting. Even if the goals of therapy have not been reached, it is appropriate to terminate therapy if it is clear that the client is not benefiting from treatment. Further deterioration of functioning is a clear indication of treatment failure. A lack of improvement in symptoms may or may not indicate a lack of benefit from treatment; if a client entered therapy on a downward trend, simply stabilizing them and keeping them out of hospitalization can be considered a benefit. Ultimately, though, clients should experience a benefit from being in therapy. If, by their own report or by therapist or other observation of client behavior, they are not improving, termination should be considered – with referrals given if symptoms still warrant treatment.

Managing termination. It is generally understood that a good termination process starts at the beginning of therapy, with therapist and client reaching clear agreement on what the goals of therapy are and what improvements will lead to a determination that therapy can end. Discussions of progress toward termination should be a regular part of therapy. Once it is clear that termination is appropriate, a responsible MFT will provide advance notice of termination, and in one or more termination sessions, the MFT will take steps to prevent a relapse of symptoms, recognize the gains the client has made in therapy, and provide appropriate referrals for any additional needed care.

Preventing abandonment or neglect. A termination process that is done too quickly or without appropriate referrals can be considered client abandonment. There may be times when a therapist does need to end therapy abruptly, either due to a medical illness, client job transfer or deployment, or for other reasons. In such circumstances, the MFT (or, in the case of the MFT's illness, someone designated by the MFT) should offer as much advance notice of termination as possible, make appropriate referrals, and follow up to ensure the clients are able to obtain continued services.

Sample Questions
See the next page for answers and rationales

1. The client of an MFT is struggling with the decision of whether to leave her 17-year marriage. The couple have had a few instances of violence, though none in the past year. Both the client and her spouse have had multiple affairs. They are struggling financially and have three young children. During a particularly frustrating session, the client throws up her hands and asks, "What do I do?" The MFT should:

    a. Answer the question directly, based on the MFT's knowledge and experience, so as to maintain the therapeutic relationship

    b. Reflect the client's struggle and her frustration at the lack of clear answers

    c. Inform the client of the overall divorce rate in her culture to better inform her decision

    d. Refer the client to an attorney to address the legal matter

2. A client asks whether her 75-year-old mother can be part of her therapy. The mother speaks English, but can only read and write in her native language, which you as the therapist are not familiar with. You believe that including the mother in the therapy may be helpful to the client. You should:

    a. Have the mother sign your informed consent form and join the therapy.

    b. Verbally discuss the process, risks, and benefits of therapy with the mother to help her decide whether to join the therapy, and document the discussion and her response.

    c. Refer the mother to a therapist who speaks her native language, and ask the client to sign a Release of Information form authorizing you to speak to that therapist.

    d. Ask the mother to teach you her native language so that you can provide all appropriate paperwork in her language.

Sample Questions: Answers and Rationales

1. The client of an MFT is struggling with the decision of whether to leave her 17-year marriage. The couple have had a few instances of violence, though none in the past year. Both the client and her spouse have had multiple affairs. They are struggling financially and have three young children. During a particularly frustrating session, the client throws up her hands and asks, "What do I do?" The MFT should:

   a. **Incorrect.** Answer the question directly, based on the MFT's knowledge and experience, so as to maintain the therapeutic relationship.
   b. **CORRECT.** Reflect the client's struggle and her frustration at the lack of clear answers.
   c. **Incorrect.** Inform the client of the overall divorce rate in her culture to better inform her decision. *While it arguably does not inform her specific decision, to whatever degree it does, it*
   d. **Incorrect.** Refer the client to an attorney to address the legal matter.

Professional codes of ethics specifically prohibit therapists from making major life decisions for their clients (A). A referral to an attorney (D) would be seen as the MFT pushing for divorce, and simply describing the divorce rate in the client's demographic group (C) suggests that the client's decision should be based on social norms rather than the client's best interests. The client here is likely expressing frustration rather than asking for a simple answer. The therapist is ethically prohibited from making the decision for the client, and is encouraged instead to help the client examine her options and the likely outcomes of each. Option (B) follows this path.

2. A client asks whether her 75-year-old mother can be part of her therapy. The mother speaks English, but can only read and write in her native language, which you as the therapist are not familiar with. You believe that including the mother in the therapy may be helpful to the client. You should:

    a. **Incorrect.** Have the mother sign your informed consent form and join the therapy.

    b. **CORRECT.** Verbally discuss the process, risks, and benefits of therapy with the mother to help her decide whether to join the therapy, and document the discussion and her response.

    c. **Incorrect.** Refer the mother to a therapist who speaks her native language, and ask the client to sign a Release of Information form authorizing you to speak to that therapist.

    d. **Incorrect.** Ask the mother to teach you her native language so that you can provide all appropriate paperwork in her language.

Consent for therapy should be documented, but the client's consent does not need to be in writing. Such a requirement would make it impossible to work with clients who are illiterate. A verbal conversation is the best way to ensure that the mother is truly able to exercise her autonomy and provide informed consent for treatment. A is incorrect because the mother's signature would not mean much on a form she could not understand. C is incorrect because it would not fulfill the request of the client, to have the mother be part of the client's therapy, which you also believe may be helpful. D is incorrect because this would be both time-consuming and a potentially inappropriate dual relationship.

ETHICS

Business Practices and Policies

Scored exam questions (approximate): 7-8

Advertising K95-97

Accurate representation. Ethically, you can only advertise those degrees or credentials you have actually earned, and which are relevant to the practice of marriage and family therapy. If you have a master's degree in family therapy and a doctorate in English, you could not include your doctorate as a professional qualification. Even though you do have a doctorate, it would be a misrepresentation of the credentials you hold relative to your clinical work.

Testimonials. The AAMFT Codes of Ethics prohibits seeking testimonials from current clients. The new CAMFT code, on the other hand, allows the practice, so long as the client is not "vulnerable to undue influence." Given this conflict, you're unlikely to see scored items on this issue on your exam, unless the issue arises in a context where a single correct answer would apply regardless of whether you are looking at the AAMFT or CAMFT codes.

Clients may feel unduly pressured by these requests. This issue has gotten more complicated in the age of Yelp, Angie's List, HealthGrades, and similar web sites designed for patients to share their experiences with a variety of professionals. Clients sometimes provide testimonials on such sites without being prompted to by therapists. MFTs should be aware that *responding* to any online testimonial may be considered a breach of client confidentiality, even when the client is openly discussing their treatment.

Recruiting clients through affiliations. As you would expect, MFTs cannot advertise themselves as being partners or associates of a group that they don't actually belong to. As with other rules about how you represent yourself, even implying an affiliation that doesn't exist, without outright saying it, would still be a violation.

Documentation K98-100

Documentation of services. Recall from earlier that neither state law nor professional ethical codes define the specific *content* that needs to be in treatment records, and there are a wide variety of formats for things like assessments and progress notes. However, all MFTs are legally required to keep records that are consistent with "sound clinical judgment, the standards of the profession, and the nature of the services being rendered" (CA BPC 4982(v)).

Professional ethical codes demand that treatment and financial records be accurate and adequate. The AAMFT and CAMFT codes of ethics both demand that MFTs document the following:

- Authorization to release confidential information
- Precautions taken regarding multiple relationships
- When client requests for records are refused, the request and reasons for refusal should both be documented
- Specific consent for recording sessions or third-party observation (must be in writing)
- Consent to share confidential and identifiable information in consultations (must be in writing)
- Consent from subjects of evaluations (must be in writing)
- Consent for use of clinical materials in teaching, writing, or presenting, unless client identities are protected

The CAMFT code also requires MFTs to document their treatment decisions, and encourages MFTs to document any agreements made by members of a therapy group to respect the confidentiality of the group.

Records should be released when legally required or permitted, when the MFT is the subject of a lawsuit or disciplinary action arising from the therapy, or when a client specifically authorizes the release in writing. Whenever records are released, the specific information released should be limited to just that which is necessary to address the specific reason for release.

Protecting the confidentiality of records. MFTs have an ethical responsibility to store, transfer, exchange, and dispose of records in ways that protect the confidentiality of those records. Methods for protecting the confidentiality of records include:

- Keeping paper records in a secure, locked file cabinet
- Keeping electronic records in a secure, encrypted format
- Carefully controlling who has access to client files
- Shredding paper files to dispose of them

Maintenance and disposal of records. During the time you are maintaining records, of course you must take reasonable steps to ensure they are secure and confidential. When the time comes that you dispose of old client records, this disposal must also be done in a manner that protects security and confidentiality. An MFT should never simply throw old client files in the trash.

Telehealth. Under California law, therapists who offer services via telemedicine are legally required to first obtain specific consent for telemedicine (the consent can be verbal or in writing) and document this in the client's file. Failure to do so is considered unprofessional conduct. While simply scheduling sessions by phone or email would not qualify as telehealth, providing therapy by phone may qualify, and providing therapy via videoconference certainly would. (Note that throughout this book, "telemedicine" and "telehealth" are used interchangeably.)

Other professional roles K101-103

Responsibility to clarify role. MFTs often serve in professional capacities that are different from being a therapist or supervisor. For example, MFTs may serve as custody evaluators, expert witnesses, consultants, or in other roles. When doing so, it is important that MFTs be clear (with everyone: themselves, clients, courts, and anyone else directly involved) about what their role is, how it is different from therapy, and how information from clients may be used and shared with the court or with other professionals.

Conflicting roles. MFTs are responsible for clearly distinguishing between the roles of therapist and evaluator. In the therapist role, an MFT is working clinically with clients to help them achieve therapeutic goals. In an evaluator role, the MFT is to remain objective, simply assessing an individual or family's functioning.

MFTs are specifically discouraged from serving as both therapist and evaluator for the same clients, unless the therapist is required to do so by a court or other legal authority. The most common example of this is custody evaluation: An MFT can be the treating therapist for a family, or be a custody evaluator for them, but not both.

The AAMFT Code of Ethics standard 7.7 prohibits MFTs from providing "evaluations for custody, residence, or visitation" for minors that the MFT has treated.

Of course, MFTs who have proper releases of information can inform the court of a minor's or family's progress in therapy. The MFT just needs to be very careful to not include statements that might be considered as evaluative statements related to custody, visitation, or whatever legal proceeding is underway.

Legal proceedings. MFTs who take part in legal proceedings have an ethical responsibility to remain impartial and objective. If your client has given you permission to testify on their behalf in a court case, you are testifying as a fact witness – someone directly involved with one of the parties in the case. Your role is not to advocate on the client's behalf, it is to accurately and objectively answer the questions put before you.

If someone has hired you solely for the purpose of providing expert knowledge to the court, but you do not have any knowledge of the people directly involved in the case, you are testifying as an expert witness. When an MFT testifies as an expert witness, the MFT must base their conclusions on sound clinical judgment and appropriate data, and must acknowledge the limitations of their data and conclusions.

When an MFT gives any professional opinion in a legal proceeding, regardless of what type of witness they role the MFT is in, their testimony must be truthful and not misleading.

Many MFTs have gotten into trouble for writing a letter to a court, or testifying in court, in a way that can be construed as assessing or diagnosing someone the MFT has never actually met. For example, MFTs have been disciplined for making evaluative statements about one parent's fitness for custody when the therapist only ever met with the other parent. The ethical guidelines for MFTs are very clear that MFTs are not to offer opinions about people that the MFT has not personally worked with.

Technology K104-106

Ethical standards. The 2015 AAMFT Code of Ethics added a number of specific requirements for therapists providing services via telemedicine, and the new CAMFT code is largely consistent with these requirements. Remember that these obligations operate *on top of* all of the regular ethical requirements for therapy, not in place of them. Therapists providing services via telemedicine are ethically obligated to:

- Ensure that their use of technology is legally compliant
- Determine that the use of technology is clinically appropriate, considering client needs and abilities
- Inform clients of the risks and benefits of telemedicine, including risks related to confidentiality, clinical limitations, emergency response, and technology failure
- Ensure the security of the communication medium
- Only use telemedicine if the MFT has appropriate training, education, or supervision in the technology being used

Limitations of telemedicine. The use of technology to connect with clients over great distances comes with some natural risks and limitations, some of which are directly addressed in the ethical requirements listed above. Some clients (and some therapists) lack the technical skills needed to use technology in the delivery of mental health services. The technology may not be sufficient for the MFT to pick up on subtle cues that would otherwise be important to assess. The client may need services beyond what the therapist can provide through telemedicine. And of course, there is always the possibility that the technology will simply fail, leaving client and therapist disconnected. While technology may be a suitable method for working with many clients, MFTs must carefully assess whether telemedicine services are appropriate to the client's needs and abilities.

Potential for harm. Taking these concerns a step further, The use of technology in therapy has the potential to harm the client or the therapeutic relationship. Direct harm may come to the client if the MFT is unable to accurately assess the nature or severity of client symptoms, or changes to those symptoms, when seeing a client by phone or online. The client also may be harmed if the therapist is unable to provide needed local resources in an emergency, or if a session taking place by phone or Internet leads to breaches of confidentiality. Even when the client is not directly harmed, the relationship between therapist and client can be damaged when technology is not used responsibly. Clients may perceive that the therapist is not as attendant to their needs, or unable to intervene with them in the ways they would in person. Unless a client is well-motivated for technology-based services, the MFT should carefully consider whether seeing the client in person would be a better fit.

Setting and collecting fees K107-111

Determining fees. There are many factors you can consider when setting fees, such as a client's income, the fees generally charged for services in your area, your own qualifications, and so on. There are three particular things you *can't* do when determining fees:

- You can't enter into an agreement with other independent practitioners or clinics to set a common fee (or common minimum fee) in your area. This would be a violation of federal antitrust law.
- You can't set different fees based on race, national origin, or any other protected class in anti-discrimination rules.
- You can't set fees that are exploitive (i.e., high fees that take advantage of clients' vulnerability or wealth).

You can raise or lower fees whenever you wish, even for existing clients. You simply need to make sure that your fee changes are within the rules listed above, and that clients have been given adequate notice of the change. There is no specific ethical standard for how long is "adequate."

You have an ethical requirement to inform clients in advance of fees that will be charged for non-therapy services, like copying records, testifying in court, or missed appointments. Remember that you also have a legal requirement to inform clients of fees and their basis prior to starting treatment.

Fees for referrals. In addition to the ethical prohibition you read about earlier, MFTs are also ethically prohibited from giving or receiving fees for referrals. It doesn't matter whether those fees come from the client or from the person you are making the referral to – both would be considered unethical. Referrals should always be made solely on the basis of the best interests of the client. If you are receiving payment for referrals, it gives the appearance that you might be giving specific referrals because there's a financial incentive for you.

Bartering. Bartering – that is, exchanging clinical services for some other product or service, rather than money – comes with a lot of potential problems. There is risk of exploitation if the market value of the goods or services the client offers as payment exceeds the usual fee the MFT charges. There is also the risk that the therapy relationship will be impacted, if the therapist particularly likes or dislikes the goods or services received, or if they hold strong sentimental value for the client.

In spite of those problems, bartering is not completely prohibited. While MFTs ordinarily do not exchange goods or services from clients in return for the MFT's clinical services – that word, "ordinarily," is used in both the AAMFT and CAMFT codes – it may be ethically acceptable in very limited circumstances. Under both the AAMFT and CAMFT Codes of Ethics, bartering with clients is *only* acceptable if all of these conditions are met:

1, The client requests it
2, The bartering is not exploitive
3, The professional relationship is not negatively impacted; and
4, A clear written bartering agreement is established.

Therapists are also encouraged to consider the cultural issues involved, such as whether bartering is an accepted practice in the community. As a general rule, you should not enter into a bartering arrangement with clients. However, under the limited circumstances described above, there may be times when bartering for services is preferable to interrupting or discontinuing treatment.

Collecting unpaid balances. MFTs are within their legal rights and ethical boundaries to collect unpaid balances, and even to use collection agencies or courts when necessary to do so. The ethics codes require that MFTs simply give clients reasonable notice before referring for collection or filing a legal claim. Naturally, the collection agency or court should not be given any clinical information about the client.

Continuation of treatment. The CAMFT Code of Ethics goes so far as to specifically *allow* termination of therapy based on non-payment of fees, so long as the termination is handled in a manner that is clinically appropriate. But when an MFT is unable or unwilling, for any reason, to provide continued care to a client, the MFT must assist the client in making arrangements for continuation of treatment.

Services paid for by a third party K112

Ethical standards for providing services when interacting with third-party payors. Insurance fraud is a legal issue. At the same time, MFTs are also ethically obligated to be truthful and accurate in documentation submitted to third-party payors. Additional ethical rules around MFTs' interactions with third-party payors include:

- Disclose to clients what information is likely to be shared with third-party payors, and obtain consent for information sharing where needed
- Explain at the beginning of therapy what the process is for collecting payment in the event that third-party coverage is denied
- Do not withhold records or information simply because you have not yet been paid for services

- Do not limit discussions of treatment alternatives to only those alternatives that will be covered by insurance or other third-party payors

When considering these standards, it is worth bearing in mind that insurance companies are not the only third-party payors with whom you may interact. Other family members sometimes pay for services. The client's workplace, another person's liability insurance (after a car accident where that other person was at fault, for example), a charitable organization, or anyone else may be paying for your client's treatment. The ethical rules around third-party payors apply to all third-party payors, not just the client's insurance company.

Gifts K113-114

While some ethical standards have gotten more strict over time, the standards around giving and receiving gifts have actually grown more flexible. This is due largely to increased recognition of the cultural significance of gifts in many populations. Refusing a small gift may be culturally insensitive. The current AAMFT Code of Ethics requires MFTs to "attend to cultural norms when considering whether to accept gifts from or give gifts to clients." We consider the effect of giving or receiving the gift on the client, and the potential impact of the gift on the therapy process. The new CAMFT Code of Ethics offers similar guidance.

Giving a gift to a client, or accepting a gift from a client, does come with some risks. The client might perceive that the gift changes the nature of their relationship with you to a more personal one. They might hold an expectation that any gift should be reciprocated. They might expect preferential treatment in scheduling or other elements of therapy. In each of these instances (and surely many others you could come up with), the integrity of the therapeutic process can be impacted. Whether you accept or reject a client gift, it is good practice to document your decision-making on the issue. You might consider factors like the cost, nature, and meaning of the gift, how it fits within cultural norms, and its potential impact on therapy.

Research ethics K115-118

Procedures for safeguarding research participants. The most important safeguard for research participants is the process of informed consent. Just as a client should be fully informed of the processes, risks, and potential benefits of therapy, a research participant should be fully informed of the processes, risks, and benefits of their participation in a study. Most studies are overseen by some form of Institutional Review Board, which reviews the protocols and protections the researchers have in place. The MFT codes of ethics also require MFTs to seek the advice of qualified colleagues in designing and conducting research, and to observe appropriate research safeguards.

Necessary disclosures to research participants. Under the CAMFT and AAMFT Codes of Ethics, research participants need to be informed of all elements of the research that you might expect to influence the participant's willingness to participate. This would include potential risks or negative effects from participating, and discomfort that the participant might be expected to go through in the study. The AAMFT Code of Ethics also requires that research participants be specifically informed of:

- Purpose of the research
- Expected length of study participation
- Study procedures
- Potential research benefits
- Limits of confidentiality
- Whom to contact with any questions about the research of their rights

Client rights when participating in research. In addition to the right to be informed about the study they are participating in, clients also have the right to decline or withdraw their participation in a study at any time. They also have a right to confidentiality unless they sign a waiver specifically authorizing the release of information from their participation. (If the study is a study involving therapy services, the same limits of confidentiality would apply as ordinarily apply in therapy, and the clients should be informed of this as part of the informed consent process.)

Confidentiality of research data. Unless clients provide a written waiver, MFTs consider any information they learn about a research participant to be confidential, subject to the exceptions to confidentiality outlined earlier. If a participant's family members or others may be able to gain access to a participant's research data, the MFT must explain this possibility at the beginning of the study and share their plan for protecting confidentiality.

Unethical or incompetent colleagues K119-120

MFTs not only need to be able to recognize when their own ability to provide therapy is compromised. We also must be aware of times when a colleague's ability to provide ethical and effective therapy is compromised. **Situations that can impair the integrity or effectiveness of therapy** include multiple relationships (subject to the boundaries previously described); therapist substance abuse, mental illness, or emotional disturbance; bias or discrimination by the therapist; exploitation; and many more.

Unlike some other states, **California does not have any rules allowing practitioners to directly report colleagues who are behaving in unethical or incompetent ways.** So when a client tells you about bad behavior on the part of their previous therapist, you are required to keep this information confidential. Reporting it to the board yourself, or directly confronting the colleague, would be an illegal and unethical breach of confidentiality. If a client grants permission for you to talk with the other therapist (through a written release of information), you could then address the other therapist, but it would be important to avoid taking the client's report at face value. There are often two very different sides to such stories, and therapists are expected to treat each other with respect.

If you learn of another therapist's illegal or incompetent behavior *directly from that therapist*, it can be more complicated. For example, if you learn that a colleague in your clinic is struggling with an alcohol abuse problem, you could encourage your colleague to seek treatment and to discontinue seeing clients until the problem is under control. The CAMFT Code of Ethics encourages MFTs to **offer assistance to colleagues who**

are impaired by substance abuse or mental or emotional problems. Doing so would certainly be in the best interests of their clients. If the other therapist refuses, though, there is no law or ethical standard that requires or even allows you to report the colleague to the board, or to take any other action. In fact, the CAMFT Code of Ethics requires therapists to **respect the confidences of colleagues** when in the context of their professional relationship.

There is only one situation that calls for specific action on your part based on another therapist's incompetence: When there has been **a sexual relationship between that therapist and their client**. In that situation, you are legally required to provide your client with the state-authored brochure called *Therapy Never Includes Sexual Behavior*. Failure to do so is unprofessional conduct, as noted above. Even when you're supplying this brochure, though, you cannot report the other therapist's conduct to the board. You can, however, encourage your client to do so.

What is most important in a situation like this is that you take appropriate action to promote the welfare of clients. While you may not report it yourself when a client tells you that another therapist is behaving unethically or incompetently, you can (and often should) encourage the client to report that behavior themselves. You can't *require* the client to make that report – that would be putting your wishes above the client's – but you can encourage it.

Supervision K121

Supervisors have a number of specific responsibilities defined in the CAMFT Code of Ethics. In brief, supervisors are required to:

- Maintain their supervision skills, getting consultation when needed
- Stay up to date in their knowledge of the practice of MFT
- Stay aware of changes to legal and ethical guidelines
- Keep supervisees aware of changes to legal and ethical guidelines
- Address cultural and diversity issues in supervision
- Have clear policies and procedures that are given to supervisees at the beginning of supervision
- Regularly evaluate supervisees, identifying concerns

- Follow the law regarding business and employment practices
- Guide supervisees in getting assistance for problems that might be hurting their work
- Document decisions to let go of supervisees
- Review trainee agreements with universities

Supervisees, meanwhile, also have a number of specific responsibilities defined in the CAMFT Code of Ethics:

- Understand that the clients the supervisee sees are considered clients of their employer
- Know the laws and regulations governing MFT practice and licensing
- Function within the limits of a supervisee's role as defined by law
- Maintain registration as required by law

The AAMFT Code of Ethics further requires that supervisees be specifically informed of the risks and benefits of technology when supervision is going to involve the use of technology.

Sample Questions
See the next page for answers and rationales

1. An MFT is planning a conference presentation, and is interested in using clips from client sessions to support the arguments she will be making about ways to address anxiety in session. She has been recording client sessions routinely with client permission for years, and describes this recording in her intake paperwork as being for supervision and consultation purposes. Prior to using the recordings at the conference, the MFT should:

   a. Seek specific permission from clients for this use of their session recordings
   b. Inform clients about the upcoming presentation
   c. Assign fake names to clients for use when discussing their specific cases
   d. Offer to provide the clients a small payment in exchange for rights to their sessions

2. A client enthusiastically tells her MFT that she was recently able to get a large supply of office paper for no cost. A local office supply store she frequents has been offering a sale where reams of paper are deeply discounted, and the manufacturer also offers a rebate on that paper. The rebate is greater than the sale price, so the customer winds up making money on the purchase. The client encourages the MFT to "stock up and get yourself some spending money too!" The client assures the MFT that the process is fully legal, and even promoted by the store. The MFT should:

   a. Take advantage of the sale if the MFT chooses.
   b. Treat the paper as a gift from the client, and accept only a small amount.
   c. Remind the client of the limits of confidentiality, and that criminal acts are not protected by privilege.
   d. Wait for the client to have been done with therapy for two years, and then see whether the offer remains available.

Sample Questions: Answers and Rationales

1. An MFT is planning a conference presentation, and is interested in using clips from client sessions to support the arguments she will be making about ways to address anxiety in session. She has been recording client sessions routinely with client permission for years, and describes this recording in her intake paperwork as being for supervision and consultation purposes. Prior to using the recordings at the conference, the MFT should:

    a. **CORRECT.** Seek specific permission from clients for this use of their session recordings

    b. **Incorrect.** Inform clients about the upcoming presentation

    c. **Incorrect.** Assign fake names to clients for use when discussing their specific cases

    d. **Incorrect.** Offer to provide the clients a small payment in exchange for rights to their sessions

While the clients have previously consented to having their sessions recorded, the MFT had specified that those recordings were for supervision and consultation purposes. It's not reasonable to put a conference presentation into that category; a conference audience is not there to provide supervision or consultation. Since the clips are being used in support of a particular conclusion, this is best considered within a research context. A conference presentation may bring forth additional risks of the clients being identified; even using fake names for them (C) would not be adequate to protect confidentiality when the audience will be able to see their faces and hear their voices on the video. Offering payment (D) is not legally or ethically necessary, and simply informing clients of the intended use (B) is not adequate. The MFT should seek new consent for this different use of session recordings (A).

2. A client enthusiastically tells her MFT that she was recently able to get a large supply of office paper for no cost. A local office supply store she frequents has been offering a sale where reams of paper are deeply discounted, and the manufacturer also offers a rebate on that paper. The rebate is greater than the sale price, so the customer winds up making money on the purchase. The client encourages the MFT to "stock up and get yourself some spending money too!" The client assures the MFT that the process is fully legal, and even promoted by the store. The MFT should:

    a. **CORRECT.** Take advantage of the sale if the MFT chooses.
    b. **Incorrect.** Treat the paper as a gift from the client, and accept only a small amount.
    c. **Incorrect.** Remind the client of the limits of confidentiality, and that criminal acts are not protected by privilege.
    d. **Incorrect.** Wait for the client to have been done with therapy for two years, and then see whether such an offer remains available.

The client is not asking the MFT to become involved in a crime (C) or engage in a sexual relationship (D). Since the client endures no direct cost, receives no direct benefit, and indeed would have no direct knowledge of whether the MFT makes use of the offer, it does not make sense to conceptualize this as a gift (B); even if it did, ethical standards do not require the therapist to accept only a small amount. Since the therapeutic relationship would not be impacted and the MFT's clinical judgment would not be in question here, the MFT is free to pursue this offer if they choose.

Batting Practice

A few more sample questions

The exam itself will not simply ask you to recount facts from the preceding pages. Instead, it will ask you to *apply and integrate* the legal and ethical standards that govern the field. That's why the sample questions so far have taken the form of case vignettes instead of simple memorization. Over the next few pages, you'll get some more practice.

What makes these questions a bit different (and, indeed, a bit tougher) from the ones you've seen already is that they ask you to combine multiple areas of knowledge when determining the correct answer. You may need to pull from several content areas to rule out incorrect responses and determine the correct one.

These next 15 questions aren't meant to be a sample test, just a handful of items to give you a sense of how knowledge might be organized and applied to arrive at the right answers here. In each question, assume you are an MFT acting within your professional role. Remember that, as is the case on the test itself, questions may be complex, and they may require careful reading – but they aren't designed to trick. There's a single, best answer for each question.

1. As a client leaves an MFT's office, the MFT believes the client poses a serious danger to the client's spouse. (The client had been making threats in session about what he would do to her.) The MFT, knowing the couple lives roughly 30 minutes from the MFT's office, calls the client immediately, and is able to resolve the danger. The client disavows any continued plan to harm his spouse, and apologizes to the MFT for "getting so out of hand." What does the MFT need to do to resolve the MFT's legal responsibility?

    a. Notify the spouse and law enforcement immediately
    b. Notify the spouse immediately
    c. Notify law enforcement within 24 hours
    d. Notify the local child protective services agency

2. An MFT is working with a same-sex couple in therapy. One partner expresses that he is feeling hostile toward the MFT. The MFT asks to meet briefly with that partner alone. During the individual discussion, the partner says that he feels the MFT is siding against him, interrupting him, and generally not respecting his complaints about the relationship. The MFT is surprised by this, and begins to wonder what else the MFT has been missing in session. How should the MFT handle their responsibilities in this case?

    a. Recognize each individual as a unique client, and offer to see the partners individually if they prefer.
    b. Discontinue treatment, as the therapeutic relationship has been corrupted, and refer to at least three therapists competent in working with same-sex couples.
    c. Conceptualize the client's reaction as paranoia, as it is inconsistent with the therapist's experience. Integrate this into the MFT's understanding of the dynamics of the relationship.
    d. Work to restore the therapeutic relationship with the partner, and consider finding consultation or supervision for this case

3. You are working with a Latina mother and her 7-year-old son in therapy, when you observe unusual bruises on the boy's face and arms. The bruises seem to be in several different stages of healing. When you ask how he got the bruises, both the boy and his mother refuse to answer. You should:

   a. Report suspected child abuse.
   b. Consider whether physical discipline is common in Latin cultures.
   c. Remind the mother of the limits of confidentiality.
   d. Ask the child to remove his shirt to inspect his torso for additional injuries.

4. A client requests and receives a copy of her clinical record from the MFT who has been providing her with therapy. The client reviews the record and becomes visibly angry, demanding that the MFT change the diagnosis in her file. The MFT should:

   a. Remind the client that treatment records are the property of the therapist.
   b. Remind the client that the MFT was not required to turn over the record at all.
   c. Remind the client that she may submit a written statement disputing the diagnosis and have that statement included in the file.
   d. Remind the client that the diagnosis is used simply to facilitate payment for services.

5. A new MFT is struggling with a difficult family case. The family consists of a same-sex couple with three children, and the parents of one of the partners. The family is experiencing behavioral problems with two of the children. The couple is deeply religious and is skeptical of therapy. The parents of one of the partners are pushing for therapy and even offering to pay for it, but the couple is concerned about the parents dictating the course of treatment or asking for services that they do not want the children to receive based on the couple's religious values. The MFT should:

    a. Consult with colleagues who have experience with family conflict over religion impacting treatment.
    b. Consult with colleagues who have experience with same-sex couples.
    c. Consult with colleagues who have experience with family conflict over religion impacting treatment and with same-sex couples.
    d. Consult with colleagues who have experience with multigenerational families.

6. An MFT working with a young adult woman learns from the woman that her ex-husband is volatile and has been drinking heavily. The woman believes that her ex-husband is planning an act of violence against his workplace. The MFT should:

    a. Attempt to warn the victims and notify police.
    b. Take reasonable steps to protect the client.
    c. Move toward hospitalization of the ex-husband.
    d. Encourage the client to notify police.

7. A married couple seeing an MFT in hopes of improving their marriage tells the therapist that they are considering taking Ecstasy together. They report having heard about users experiencing moments of great bonding while using the drug. They ask the MFT whether she would recommend the couple try it together, and make clear that they would be using the drug in their home without anyone else present. Ethically, the MFT should:

    a. Discourage all forms of lawbreaking, including illegal drug use.
    b. Review with the clients how they perceive the possible risks and benefits.
    c. Refer all discussion of drug effects to a physician.
    d. Update the diagnosis of one or both partners to include Substance Use Disorder.

8. An investigator with a federal law enforcement agency shows up unexpectedly at an LMFT's office. The investigator says she is looking into suspicious behavior by an individual the investigator knows is seeing the LMFT. The investigator demands access to all information the LMFT has about the client, and says that the investigation is related to national security. The LMFT should:

    a. Provide access to the records, and not inform the client she has done so.
    b. Provide access to the records, and immediately inform the client she has done so.
    c. Deny access to the records until she can contact the client and determine the client's wishes.
    d. Deny access to the records and assert privilege on behalf of the client.

9. The client of an MFT notices that before her session, as the MFT is escorting her previous appointment out of the office, the MFT and the person she is escorting out are discussing plans to have coffee together later. The client asks the MFT about this at the beginning of her session. The client tells the MFT that she, too, would like to have a more personal and social relationship with the therapist that involves meeting outside of the office. What should the MFT do to manage her ethical responsibilities in this case?

    a. Consider whether the earlier appointment was confidential.
    b. Inform the client that the existing relationship is not unethical as it has no negative impact on client care. Consider whether a similar relationship is possible with the current client.
    c. Scold the client for inquiring about the therapist's relationships.
    d. Cancel the coffee plan by phone with the client in the room, to acknowledge and take responsibility for her mistake.

10. A 13-year-old girl presents for treatment at a nonprofit agency that provides no-cost therapy. The girl is assigned to an MFT. The MFT determines the girl is not in crisis. The girl says she is suffering from distress related to family conflict. Legally, the appropriate first step for the MFT at this point is to:

    a. Contact the girl's parents to seek consent for treatment
    b. Assess the girl's emotional maturity
    c. Proceed with therapy, and involve the girl's parents
    d. Assess whether the girl is engaging in substance abuse

11. An MFT in a cash-pay private practice notices that several clients have unpaid balances. Some of those with unpaid balances attend the same religious service as the MFT. As the MFT considers how to resolve the unpaid balances, how can the MFT best address their legal responsibilities?

   a. Forgive the balances of those in the religious group, and consider it a donation to that group.
   b. Terminate the clients with unpaid balances above $250, refusing to release records or provide other documentation or referrals until the balance is paid.
   c. Work with each client with an unpaid balance to develop a payment plan.
   d. Charge fees for unpaid balances, to discourage clients from carrying balances in the future. Inform all clients of the new fee and how much, if any, they additionally owe.

12. An MFT is working as part of a treatment team in a county-run clinic. A colleague who is providing group therapy to clients in need of social skills training voices concern about one of the clients in the group. The client's attendance has become sporadic, and their behavior in group has varied from hyperactive to nearly silent. The client's case manager notes that medication compliance has sometimes been an issue for this client in the past. The MFT should:

   a. Offer to take over the social skills group to better assess the client
   b. Reconsider the client's diagnosis
   c. Ensure that conclusions about the client's medication compliance are made only by medical professionals
   d. Share what the MFT is aware of about the client's family and social context

13. "This would be the third time I've quit a job in 10 months," a queer client tells their MFT in an individual session. "I wonder whether I'm self-sabotaging." The MFT notes the client's lifelong pattern of self-sabotage, and provides examples. The client only becomes more insistent that quitting their job, which is the client's only source of income, is the right thing to do. As they discuss further, the client – who recently entered into a new relationship, and who moved into a new apartment four months ago – tells the MFT they are considering moving out of state to be closer to family. The MFT should:

    a. Use the opportunity to challenge the client's decision-making
    b. Discuss the potential impacts of these choices on the client
    c. Connect the client's self-sabotage with their queer identity
    d. Consider whether the client's erratic behavior warrants possible hospitalization

14. An MFT is at a concert, and sees a teenage client at the concert with a friend. The client and the friend both appear to be intoxicated. At one point toward the end of the concert, the client notices the MFT, and quickly puts her head down in embarrassment. How should the MFT address their ethical responsibilities?

    a. Walk up to the client, without revealing their relationship, and say something along the lines of, "You're allowed to have fun." At the next scheduled session, pretend she did not see the client at all.
    b. Leave the concert, and consider terminating therapy as the integrity of the therapeutic relationship has been corrupted. The therapist's judgment is no longer based solely on clinical information.
    c. Stay at the concert, avoid further contact with the client, and inform the client's parents of what the MFT observed.
    d. Stay at the concert, and allow the client to determine whether they will say hello. Discuss therapeutic boundaries at the next session.

15. Your friend, who is also an MFT, tells you she has been struggling with a drinking problem since the death of her father six months ago. You should:

    a. Report the friend to the BBS, as she is unable to provide quality clinical care.

    b. Offer to provide confidential therapy to the friend to protect her clients.

    c. Encourage the friend to enter treatment for grief and substance use.

    d. Inform the friend's employer that she may not be healthy enough to provide services.

Batting practice:
Answers and rationales

As always, it's useful to carefully review not only what answers are correct and incorrect, but also *why* the various answers are right and wrong.

1. As a client leaves an MFT's office, the MFT believes the client poses a serious danger to the client's spouse. (The client had been making threats in session about what he would do to her.) The MFT, knowing the couple lives roughly 30 minutes from the MFT's office, calls the client immediately, and is able to resolve the danger. The client disavows any continued plan to harm his spouse, and apologizes to the MFT for "getting so out of hand." What does the MFT need to do to resolve the MFT's legal responsibility?

   a. **Incorrect.** Notify the spouse and law enforcement immediately
   b. **Incorrect.** Notify the spouse immediately
   c. **CORRECT.** Notify law enforcement within 24 hours
   d. **Incorrect.** Notify the local child protective services agency

While warning an intended victim in a *Tarasoff* situation grants the MFT certain additional legal protections, it is not always necessary or appropriate to do so. In this case, the MFT was able to fully resolve the threat on their own, before notifying the intended victim or law enforcement. Still, under state law, the fact that the MFT's *Tarasoff* responsibilities were triggered *at all* means that the MFT must report the threatening person to law enforcement within 24 hours, even if notifying law enforcement was not necessary to resolve the initial threat. As noted in the study guide, the idea of this law is to prevent potentially dangerous individuals from buying guns.

2. An MFT is working with a same-sex couple in therapy. One partner expresses that he is feeling hostile toward the MFT. The MFT asks to meet briefly with that partner alone. During the individual discussion, the partner says that he feels the MFT is siding against him, interrupting him, and generally not respecting his complaints about the relationship. The MFT is surprised by this, and begins to wonder what else the MFT has been missing in session. How should the MFT handle their responsibilities in this case?

- a. **Incorrect.** Recognize each individual as a unique client, and offer to see the partners individually if they prefer.
- b. **Incorrect.** Discontinue treatment, as the therapeutic relationship has been corrupted, and refer to at least three therapists competent in working with same-sex couples.
- c. **Incorrect.** Conceptualize the client's reaction as paranoia, as it is inconsistent with the therapist's experience. Integrate this into the MFT's understanding of the dynamics of the relationship.
- d. **CORRECT.** Work to restore the therapeutic relationship with the partner, and consider finding consultation or supervision for this case.

Maintaining the therapeutic relationship becomes a complex task with couples and families. Here, the MFT is surprised by a partner feeling ganged up on. The MFT should not respond by defensively discontinuing treatment (B) or dismissing the client's experience as evidence of pathology (C). Since the unit of treatment is the couple, splitting them on the basis of this exchange (A) is premature at best, and raises its own set of ethical concerns. A more appropriate first step would be to resolve this rift in the therapeutic relationship without otherwise compromising the established therapeutic process.

3. You are working with a Latina mother and her 7-year-old son in therapy, when you observe unusual bruises on the boy's face and arms. The bruises seem to be in several different stages of healing. When you ask how he got the bruises, both the boy and his mother refuse to answer. You should:

    a. **CORRECT.** Report suspected child abuse.
    b. **Incorrect.** Consider whether physical discipline is common in Latin cultures.
    c. **Incorrect.** Remind the mother of the limits of confidentiality.
    d. **Incorrect.** Ask the child to remove his shirt to inspect his torso for additional injuries.

While the injuries, and both clients' response to the therapist's inquiries, are not a guarantee that abuse has taken place, remember that the therapist does not need to be certain. They just need to reasonably suspect abuse. The location of the injuries, the fact that they are in multiple stages of healing, and the refusal to explain them would amount to reasonable suspicion in almost any MFT's mind. B would not be correct because the abuse reporting standards do not change on the basis of client culture. C is not correct because it would be an insufficient response to what appears to be abuse. D is not correct because this would place the MFT in the role of an investigator, which is not the proper role of a therapist.

4. A client requests and receives a copy of her clinical record from the MFT who has been providing her with therapy. The client reviews the record and becomes visibly angry, demanding that the MFT change the diagnosis in her file. The MFT should:

a. **Incorrect.** Remind the client that treatment records are the property of the therapist. *While it is accurate that records are the property of the therapist or their employer, that fact does not address the issue at hand.*

b. **Incorrect.** Remind the client that the MFT was not required to turn over the record at all. *The MFT does have an obligation to release a client's records unless the MFT believes that doing so will be harmful, which triggers a number of further legal obligations.*

c. **CORRECT.** Remind the client that she may submit a written statement disputing the diagnosis and have that statement included in the file. *This is a legal right of any client who disagrees with something in their record.*

d. **Incorrect.** Remind the client that the diagnosis is used simply to facilitate payment for services. *Diagnosis serves many purposes beyond facilitating payment, including the facilitation of emergency treatment and helping professionals communicate with one another.*

5. A new MFT is struggling with a difficult family case. The family consists of a same-sex couple with three children, and the parents of one of the partners. The family is experiencing behavioral problems with two of the children. The couple is deeply religious and is skeptical of therapy. The parents of one of the partners are pushing for therapy and even offering to pay for it, but the couple is concerned about the parents dictating the course of treatment or asking for services that they do not want the children to receive based on the couple's religious values. The MFT should:

    a. **CORRECT.** Consult with colleagues who have experience with family conflict over religion impacting treatment.

    b. **Incorrect.** Consult with colleagues who have experience with same-sex couples.

    c. **Incorrect.** Consult with colleagues who have experience with family conflict over religion impacting treatment and with same-sex couples.

    d. **Incorrect.** Consult with colleagues who have experience with multi-generational families.

The issue being addressed is the question of who will control treatment. The fact that the family includes a same-sex couple does not appear, from the information in the vignette, to be relevant to this particular issue. (It may, of course, but nothing in the question suggests that it is.) Consultation is not necessary over every demographic variable an MFT is confronted with, particularly when that variable does not appear to be relevant to the treatment.

6. An MFT working with a young adult woman learns from the woman that her ex-husband is volatile and has been drinking heavily. The woman believes that her ex-husband is planning an act of violence against his workplace. The MFT should:

   a. **Incorrect.** Attempt to warn the victims and notify police. Tarasoff *does not apply here, as the dangerous person is not the MFT's client.*

   b. **Incorrect.** Take reasonable steps to protect the client. *The client is aware of the threat and is not an intended victim. No protective steps appear to be needed.*

   c. **Incorrect.** Move toward hospitalization of the ex-husband. *It is not clear whether the ex-husband is a general danger to others, and the limited evidence here suggests instead that he poses a specific danger rather than a general one.*

   d. **CORRECT.** Encourage the client to notify police. *Since she has the best knowledge of his status and plans, she should inform police directly in order to address the threat.*

7. A married couple seeing an MFT in hopes of improving their marriage tells the therapist that they are considering taking Ecstasy together. They report having heard about users experiencing moments of great bonding while using the drug. They ask the MFT whether she would recommend the couple try it together, and make clear that they would be using the drug in their home without anyone else present. Ethically, the MFT should:

a. **Incorrect.** Discourage all forms of lawbreaking, including illegal drug use. *MFTs are neither required nor encouraged to discourage all forms of lawbreaking. Some lawbreaking, in some contexts, may be appropriate.*

b. **CORRECT.** Review with the clients how they perceive the possible risks and benefits. *This best preserves client autonomy and the MFT's role.*

c. **Incorrect.** Refer all discussion of drug effects to a physician. *While advising on drugs would be outside of the MFT's scope of practice, the discussion in this case does not need to involve the MFT providing medical advice. The clients can tell the MFT how the clients perceive possible risks and benefits.*

d. **Incorrect.** Update the diagnosis of one or both partners to include Substance Use Disorder. *Simple use is not the same as a use disorder, and in this case, the couple has not yet even advanced to use. A change in diagnosis is not called for.*

8. An investigator with a federal law enforcement agency shows up unexpectedly at an LMFT's office. The investigator says she is looking into suspicious behavior by an individual the investigator knows is seeing the LMFT. The investigator demands access to all information the LMFT has about the client, and says that the investigation is related to national security. The LMFT should:

    a.   **CORRECT.** Provide access to the records, and not inform the client she has done so. *MFTs can be required to turn over records in a national security investigation and cannot tell the client they have done so.*

    b.   **Incorrect.** Provide access to the records, and immediately inform the client she has done so. *Informing the client in this instance would be a violation of federal law.*

    c.   **Incorrect.** Deny access to the records until she can contact the client and determine the client's wishes. *In a national security investigation, an MFT can be required to turn over records. Denying the investigator access to the records could be a violation of federal law.*

    d.   **Incorrect.** Deny access to the records and assert privilege on behalf of the client. *In a national security investigation, an MFT can be required to turn over records. Denying the investigator access to the records could be a violation of federal law.*

9. The client of an MFT notices that before her session, as the MFT is escorting her previous appointment out of the office, the MFT and the person she is escorting out are discussing plans to have coffee together later. The client asks the MFT about this at the beginning of her session. The client tells the MFT that she, too, would like to have a more personal and social relationship with the therapist that involves meeting outside of the office. What should the MFT do to manage her ethical responsibilities in this case?

    a. **CORRECT.** Consider whether the earlier appointment was confidential.

    b. **Incorrect.** Inform the client that the existing relationship is not unethical as it has no negative impact on client care. Consider whether a similar relationship is possible with the current client.

    c. **Incorrect.** Scold the client for inquiring about the therapist's relationships.

    d. **Incorrect.** Cancel the coffee plan by phone with the client in the room, to acknowledge and take responsibility for her mistake.

We have to be careful about the assumptions we make. Therapists meet with a lot of people in our offices, not all of whom are clients. The person the MFT was escorting out of the office could have been a friend, a colleague, a business associate, or anything else. The MFT may want to be transparent with the client about the nature of that relationship, if they can legally and ethically do so. That transparency would reduce the client's concern that another client was receiving special treatment, and reinforce the boundaries of the therapist-client relationship.

10. A 13-year-old girl presents for treatment at a nonprofit agency that provides no-cost therapy. The girl is assigned to an MFT. The MFT determines the girl is not in crisis. The girl says she is suffering from distress related to family conflict. Legally, the appropriate first step for the MFT at this point is to:

a. **Incorrect.** Contact the girl's parents to seek consent for treatment
b. **CORRECT.** Assess the girl's emotional maturity
c. **Incorrect.** Proceed with therapy, and involve the girl's parents
d. **Incorrect.** Assess whether the girl is engaging in substance abuse

Minors as young as 12 can independently consent for mental health care so long as they are mature enough to participate intelligently in treatment. The MFT must make that determination to know whether consent for treatment can be present. Contacting the girl's parents to seek consent (A) would be necessary if the minor is assessed and determined not to be able to independently consent. Proceeding with therapy (C), and assessing for substance abuse (D), is appropriate after consent has been obtained.

11. An MFT in a cash-pay private practice notices that several clients have unpaid balances. Some of those with unpaid balances attend the same religious service as the MFT. As the MFT considers how to resolve the unpaid balances, how can the MFT best address their legal responsibilities?

a. **Incorrect.** Forgive the balances of those in the religious group, and consider it a donation to that group.
b. **Incorrect.** Terminate the clients with unpaid balances above $250, refusing to release records or provide other documentation or referrals until the balance is paid.
c. **CORRECT.** Work with each client with an unpaid balance to develop a payment plan.
d. **Incorrect.** Charge fees for unpaid balances, to discourage clients from carrying balances in the future. Inform all clients of the new fee and how much, if any, they additionally owe.

Forgiving the balances of those who share the MFT's religious practice, while not forgiving the balances of others (A), would likely be considered discrimination based on religion. Terminating clients for lack of payment (B) can be ethically acceptable, but must be done in a clinically responsible way. The MFT cannot refuse to release records on the basis of an unpaid balance. While it is legal to charge fees for unpaid balances (D), such fees need to be spelled out to clients *before* they are implemented -- typically in the initial informed consent agreement. Imposing them before informing clients of them would be a violation.

12. An MFT is working as part of a treatment team in a county-run clinic. A colleague who is providing group therapy to clients in need of social skills training voices concern about one of the clients in the group. The client's attendance has become sporadic, and their behavior in group has varied from hyperactive to nearly silent. The client's case manager notes that medication compliance has sometimes been an issue for this client in the past. The MFT should:

a. **Incorrect.** Offer to take over the social skills group to better assess the client
b. **Incorrect.** Reconsider the client's diagnosis
c. **Incorrect.** Ensure that conclusions about the client's medication compliance are made only by medical professionals
d. **CORRECT.** Share what the MFT is aware of about the client's family and social context

Working on a treatment team means collaborating with a variety of other professionals and recognizing each individual's skill sets. Here, there's no reason the MFT should take over the social skills group (A), as there is no evidence that there's anything missing in the colleague's assessment ability. There's also no evidence of a problem in the client's diagnosis (B), which the question doesn't even provide. Similarly, while only medical professionals can issue medical diagnoses or prescribe medication, a case manager is qualified to make determinations about medication compliance (C). Any MFT is trained at placing behavior in its family and social context (D), and that's what the MFT's contribution should be here.

13. "This would be the third time I've quit a job in 10 months," a queer client tells their MFT in an individual session. "I wonder whether I'm self-sabotaging." The MFT notes the client's lifelong pattern of self-sabotage, and provides examples. The client only becomes more insistent that quitting their job, which is the client's only source of income, is the right thing to do. As they discuss further, the client – who recently entered into a new relationship, and who moved into a new apartment four months ago – tells the MFT they are considering moving out of state to be closer to family. The MFT should:

    a. **Incorrect.** Use the opportunity to challenge the client's decision-making

    b. **CORRECT.** Discuss the potential impacts of these choices on the client

    c. **Incorrect.** Connect the client's self-sabotage with their queer identity

    d. **Incorrect.** Consider whether the client's erratic behavior warrants possible hospitalization

Let's dispose of the ridiculous first: There's nothing here to suggest danger that would warrant hospitalizations (D), and while various symptoms can be linked to various aspects of identity, there's nothing here to suggest that the client's self-sabotage has anything at all to do with their being queer (C). Challenging the client's decision-making (A) may have some clinical utility to it, but fundamentally this question is assessing your ability to support client autonomy. That ethical obligation is better addressed with (B).

14. An MFT is at a concert, and sees a teenage client at the concert with a friend. The client and the friend both appear to be intoxicated. At one point toward the end of the concert, the client notices the MFT, and quickly puts her head down in embarrassment. How should the MFT address their ethical responsibilities?

a. **Incorrect.** Walk up to the client, without revealing their relationship, and say something along the lines of, "You're allowed to have fun." At the next scheduled session, pretend she did not see the client at all.

b. **Incorrect.** Leave the concert, and consider terminating therapy as the integrity of the therapeutic relationship has been corrupted. The therapist's judgment is no longer based solely on clinical information.

c. **Incorrect.** Stay at the concert, avoid further contact with the client, and inform the client's parents of what the MFT observed.

d. **CORRECT.** Stay at the concert, and allow the client to determine whether they will say hello. Discuss therapeutic boundaries at the next session.

Clients and therapists encounter each other by chance with some regularity. This is especially common in rural areas, and among some tightly-knit communities. MFTs typically address this possibility at the beginning of therapy, or in their informed consent documents. The therapist may wish to resolve the client's embarrassment by going directly to her (A), but this would likely heighten the client's embarrassment, and may require an explanation to the friend -- needlessly risking that the therapeutic relationship would be revealed. The therapist has no ethical obligation to leave the concert (B), and terminating therapy based on this chance encounter would be premature and likely inappropriate. Informing the parents of what the MFT observed (C) would be a breach of confidentiality unless such disclosures had been explicitly agreed to at the outset of therapy, something that is not indicated in the question. The most ethically sound choice is to remain at the concert without allowing it to create a dual relationship (D), and revisiting boundaries around confidentiality at the next session.

15. Your friend, who is also an MFT, tells you she has been struggling with a drinking problem since the death of her father six months ago. You should:

    a. **Incorrect.** Report the friend to the BBS, as she is unable to provide quality clinical care.

    b. **Incorrect.** Offer to provide confidential therapy to the friend to protect her clients.

    c. **CORRECT.** Encourage the friend to enter treatment for grief and substance use.

    d. **Incorrect.** Inform the friend's employer that she may not be healthy enough to provide services

The correct answer is C. The CAMFT Code of Ethics guides MFTs to encourage struggling colleagues to receive help for issues that interfere with clinical care. We cannot, however, share this information with the BBS or the employer, as the code requires MFTs to respect the confidences of colleagues. Providing direct treatment to the friend would be an improper dual relationship.

How did you do? If you struggled a bit with these, don't worry. It's most important at this stage that you are able to understand *why* any questions you got wrong were incorrect. If you are interested in taking a full-length practice test, well, that's up next.

You've got this.

Good luck!

Taking the practice test

This test is 75 questions, the same length as the actual test. Use them as you see fit! There are a number of different ways you could use these items to help you prepare:

1. **Focus on understanding.** In this study method, you would take a practice test untimed, focusing on carefully examining the question and thinking through the available responses. You would then spend a fair amount of time with the *rationale* for each correct answer, making sure that you are deeply understanding the underlying concepts. While of course you hope to get a good score, your score on the practice exam is not terribly important when understanding is your goal. Any question you answer incorrectly is simply a chance to expand your knowledge and better prepare you for the real test. After all, while the actual test will cover the same content areas as this practice exam, it is unlikely they will ask the same questions in the same ways. You need to be able to understand and *apply* the key legal and ethical concepts across different clinical situations.

2. **Focus on timing.** In this study method, you would time yourself on the test, making sure you finish within the 90-minute time limit. This also gives you an opportunity to practice any anxiety management techniques you may need, and to practice time management skills like skipping questions you may want to come back to later. Many examinees have reported that they spent more time on the actual test than they did on practice tests, so it's good if you have at least some amount of time left over when you complete the test here.

3. **Focus on performance.** In this study method, a good score is the only goal. As is the case in method 1 above, you still want to make sure you understand why you answered incorrectly on any items you got wrong, but this method is more about confidence-building leading up to your test day. One thing to note if you're focused on your score: Because cycles of the real exam vary in difficulty, it is not safe to presume that a score on any given practice test (the one

here, or anyone else's) equates with roughly the same score on the real thing. If you're getting a significant majority of the items on a practice test right, your scores have been steadily improving, and you can understand why any incorrect answers you gave were incorrect, that is probably a better measure of preparedness than any specific score.

There are other, more creative ways you can use the material here as well, such as:

- Quizzing others in a study group
- Dividing the questions into three "mini-exams" of 25 questions each
- Using the book as a study guide, going through questions and rationales one at a time

I'm a big believer in being pragmatic where studying for an exam is concerned. Do what you know works best for you.

A few cautionary notes

While these questions and responses are written to help prepare you for the California MFT Law and Ethics Exam, it is important to bear in mind that the practice test here (like all practice tests) is an *approximation* of the style and format of the exam itself. The actual exam changes with each 90-day test cycle; some exam cycles have a difficult exam, while others have an easier exam. This is why the passing score changes with each cycle, to ensure that examinees aren't disadvantaged by happening into a tougher cycle of the test.

It's also worth noting that, while every effort has been made here to tie these questions with specific and identifiable legal and ethical principles, ethical decision-making isn't always clear-cut. Even on questions where these is a clear correct answer, reasonable arguments can sometimes be made for some of the other response choices. If you find yourself arguing with the rationale on a question, focus your efforts on understanding why the correct response was identified as such.

If you are using multiple practice tests from different sources (for example, if you are using this book alongside practice tests provided by a test prep company), you may find that in some instances, the different sources suggest different answers for similar questions. That can be confusing and anxiety-provoking, but usually has a good explanation. You may be able to find that even minor, technical differences between the questions account for the differences in the best answers. You may also find that one source or another has something wrong – either because the law or ethical standard has changed, or because it has been misinterpreted. All of us (myself included) make mistakes on occasion. Rest assured that for the actual exam, every item must be keyed to an objective standard, so there will always be a current, justifiable best answer. If you find yourself disagreeing with a practice item from any source, and you have a clear legal or ethical rationale supporting your response choice, you're probably in good shape for the actual test. And of course, if you'd like to discuss anything in this book that you think I may have incorrect, please email my team at support@BenCaldwellLabs.com and let us know.

Finally, you may find that some questions here resemble situations that you have actually encountered in your practice. Hopefully it would go without saying, but nothing here should be construed as legal advice or as a substitution for consulting with a qualified attorney. The kinds of case vignettes that are written for an exam are (by design) reductionist, focusing on only a few features of a case. Real-life decision-making is often more complex.

Answer Sheets

California MFT Law & Ethics

1. _____	21. _____	41. _____	61. _____
2. _____	22. _____	42. _____	62. _____
3. _____	23. _____	43. _____	63. _____
4. _____	24. _____	44. _____	64. _____
5. _____	25. _____	45. _____	65. _____
6. _____	26. _____	46. _____	66. _____
7. _____	27. _____	47. _____	67. _____
8. _____	28. _____	48. _____	68. _____
9. _____	29. _____	49. _____	69. _____
10. _____	30. _____	50. _____	70. _____
11. _____	31. _____	51. _____	71. _____
12. _____	32. _____	52. _____	72. _____
13. _____	33. _____	53. _____	73. _____
14. _____	34. _____	54. _____	74. _____
15. _____	35. _____	55. _____	75. _____
16. _____	36. _____	56. _____	
17. _____	37. _____	57. _____	
18. _____	38. _____	58. _____	
19. _____	39. _____	59. _____	
20. _____	40. _____	60. _____	

California MFT Law & Ethics

1. ____	21. ____	41. ____	61. ____
2. ____	22. ____	42. ____	62. ____
3. ____	23. ____	43. ____	63. ____
4. ____	24. ____	44. ____	64. ____
5. ____	25. ____	45. ____	65. ____
6. ____	26. ____	46. ____	66. ____
7. ____	27. ____	47. ____	67. ____
8. ____	28. ____	48. ____	68. ____
9. ____	29. ____	49. ____	69. ____
10. ____	30. ____	50. ____	70. ____
11. ____	31. ____	51. ____	71. ____
12. ____	32. ____	52. ____	72. ____
13. ____	33. ____	53. ____	73. ____
14. ____	34. ____	54. ____	74. ____
15. ____	35. ____	55. ____	75. ____
16. ____	36. ____	56. ____	
17. ____	37. ____	57. ____	
18. ____	38. ____	58. ____	
19. ____	39. ____	59. ____	
20. ____	40. ____	60. ____	

Practice Test

1. An MFT refers a client to a local psychiatrist for an evaluation for possible medication treatment. A few weeks later, the MFT receives a card in the mail from the psychiatrist, saying "thank you for the kind referral" and including a $10 gift card for coffee. The client's name is not mentioned anywhere. How should the MFT manage their responsibilities?

    a. Thank the psychiatrist for the gift, also without mentioning any client names

    b. Return the gift

    c. Accept the gift if the MFT chooses, as it is for a trivial amount and no confidential information was inappropriately shared

    d. Forward the gift to the client rather than accepting it directly

2. A client comes to therapy expressing concern about his 94-year-old mother. The client tells the therapist that his mother, who lives a few houses down from the client, has been refusing to eat and is unwilling to leave her home to see a doctor. She is losing weight and appears to be in declining health, but wants simply to be left alone. The client is unsure of how to help. The MFT should:

    a. Encourage the client to openly discuss his concern with his mother.

    b. Encourage the client to transport his mother to a doctor for evaluation even if it means doing so against her will.

    c. Encourage the client to report the situation to his local adult protective service agency.

    d. Report the situation to the local adult protective service agency.

3. An MFT becomes nervous when her male client, who has been struggling with symptoms of psychosis, threatens to drive his car into oncoming traffic on the way home. If the therapist believes that the client poses a threat as the client leaves the office, the MFT should:

    a.   Determine from the client's file his address and most likely route home, so that possible victims on that route can be warned.

    b.   Contact law enforcement to initiate the process of assessment for involuntary hospitalization.

    c.   Contact law enforcement to have the client arrested.

    d.   Maintain confidentiality, as the client has not threatened any identifiable victims.

4. A couple living in a rural area seeks online treatment from an MFT in a large city more than 100 miles away. The MFT specializes in infidelity, and one partner recently revealed a six-month affair. The other partner has been deeply distressed, unable to sleep since that time. During an initial phone call, the couple tells the MFT that they do not have a computer of their own, and so will be using the computer and webcam at the home of one of their parents. The MFT informs the clients of the risks and benefits of online therapy, and the couple agrees to go forward. During the first session, the MFT notices that people -- presumably the parents -- are walking by in the background, and the couple often seems uncomfortable discussing their relationship. The session is cut short when the couple accidentally disconnects the microphone, and they cannot figure out how to get it working again. Though unable to hear them, the MFT observes the couple's frustration and disappointment. The MFT should:

    a.   Schedule an in-person consultation with the couple at the MFT's office.

    b.   Ask the couple to ensure that no other people will be around when they are doing an online session.

    c.   Remind the clients of the risks and benefits of online services.

    d.   Attempt to connect the clients with qualified providers of in-person services in their area.

5. After a few sessions, a client tells an MFT that the client can no longer afford to pay for services. However, the client makes blankets and scarves at her home, bartering is common in her culture and neighborhood, and she would be willing to exchange these goods for sessions at fair market value. How should the MFT manage their ethical obligations?

    a.   Work with the client on a pro bono basis. Inform the client that the MFT would happily accept a single scarf as a gift, to protect the therapeutic relationship, but that this would be separate from any payment for services

    b.   Develop a clear contract with the client establishing the market value of the goods, when they are to be received, and how many sessions will be provided in exchange

    c.   Terminate therapy for inability to pay, and provide referrals to community resources

    d.   Allow the client to carry a balance for therapy, until such time as the client can sell enough blankets and scarves to pay for services

6. An LMFT working in an agency setting learns that a child she sees for therapy has been physically abused by the child's parents. The parents are treated by another therapist at the same agency, and it was that therapist who shared the information about the abuse and is preparing a written report to the local child protective service agency. The LMFT believes she has information from her last meeting with the child that would be relevant to the abuse report. How should the LMFT proceed?

    a.   File her own independent report of suspected child abuse, based on the information she learned from the colleague

    b.   Provide the relevant information to the colleague, and collaborate on the report

    c.   Take no action

    d.   Because the LMFT is the victim's direct therapist, ask the colleague to provide all the available information and allow the LMFT to determine what will be reported

7. A 59-year-old woman is living in a nursing home and struggling with early-onset dementia. Three of her daughters come to an MFT for family therapy to address their conflict surrounding their mother's treatment. In session, the two younger daughters say that the older daughter is refusing to let them see their mother, and does not even allow the mother to receive letters or phone calls. The older daughter acknowledges this, but says it is in everyone's best interests, as medical staff at the nursing home have informed her that the mother may not recognize her daughters. The older daughter says she is doing her best to spare everyone as much pain as she can. How should the MFT manage responsibilities in this case?

    a.   Provide family therapy to address conflict among the daughters. Request a Release of Information that would allow the MFT to speak with nursing home staff and the mother, to see whether the mother may be able to participate in some way

    b.   Ask the older daughter to verify her medical credentials that might allow her to make this determination for her family

    c.   Report suspected dependent adult abuse to the local adult protective service agency

    d.   Refer the family to an attorney to discuss power of attorney and related issues surrounding medical decision-making

8. After years of providing services in the office, an MFT decides to transition their practice to be exclusively online. The MFT selects a new videoconferencing platform that advertises itself as being secure and HIPAA-compliant. In a letter, the MFT informs all existing office clients that their care will be moved online as of roughly one month from the date of the letter. Prior to completing this transition, what must the MFT do to address their ethical responsibilities?

    a.   Terminate or refer out all in-person clients with serious symptoms

    b.   Allow the clients to choose whether they would like to continue seeing the MFT in-office rather than moving to telehealth

    c.   Take reasonable steps to identify crisis resources local to each client

    d.   Take a training on using the videoconference software

9. An MFT has been conducting telehealth sessions via video with a 23-year-old client. In the middle of a session, the client's boyfriend walks into the frame, visible to the therapist, kisses the client, and appears to leave their home to go to work. The MFT should:

  a. Discuss the risks to confidentiality when working online
  b. Ask the client to sign a Release of Information form allowing disclosure of therapeutic information, even if incidental, to the partner
  c. Ask the partner to sign a Release of Information form allowing them to receive therapeutic information
  d. Discontinue the session and, in writing, remind the client that therapy is to be conducted only from a private, confidential setting. If the client cannot find such a setting, they are inappropriate for telehealth

10. An MFT is treating a middle-aged woman whose treatment is being paid for by the client's sister. The MFT has never met or spoken with the sister. The client simply brings in a check for each session, written by her sister and made payable to the therapist. After several weeks of treatment, the sister phones the therapist and asks what the payments were being used for. "I thought she was getting medical treatment, but now she's tells me she's been spending my money on this psychobabble nonsense," the sister says. The MFT should:

  a. Argue that psychotherapy is a valid form of treatment, without discussing the client specifically.
  b. Provide limited information on the client, including service dates, diagnosis, and types of service, that the sister is legally entitled to as the payer.
  c. Offer to refund the sister's payments and collect fees directly from the client.
  d. Listen to the sister without offering any information on the client, and encourage the client to discuss the issue with her sister.

11. An MFT is planning her retirement in a few months, and has agreed to sell her private practice to a local colleague. Several weeks before she turns the practice over, the MFT should:

    a.   Inform clients of her plans, and instruct them to continue as usual with the colleague as the colleague takes over.

    b.   Inform clients of her plans, and request that each client who wishes to continue treatment with the colleague sign a Release of Information form allowing their files to be transferred.

    c.   Inform clients of her plans, and offer to do a series of transitional sessions with each client while they are simultaneously starting therapy with the colleague.

    d.   Inform clients of her plans, and draft a transition document for the colleague.

12. An MFT finds herself enjoying sessions with a high-functioning client who comes in to discuss her occasional anxiety symptoms. The MFT and client have similar tastes and similar senses of humor. The client asks whether the MFT might be interested in joining the client for lunch on a regular basis, separate from their therapy relationship. Ethically, the MFT should:

    a.   Consider whether engaging in a friendship with the client would be detrimental to the therapy.

    b.   Inform the client that they could only engage in a friendship once two years have passed since the last professional contact.

    c.   Politely refuse the offer.

    d.   Join the client for lunch on a one-time basis, in support of the therapeutic relationship.

13. After an especially difficult session with a client an MFT considers to have a personality disorder, the MFT seeks to consult with a former professor from the MFT's graduate degree program, who is now retired. The MFT plans to call the professor to ask how the professor might handle the case, including asking about specific interventions and asking about whether the MFT should consider referring the case out. Legally, the MFT should:

    a. Share specific information about the session only if they are careful not to mention the client's name
    b. Establish a written contract with the professor for the consultation
    c. Ask the client to sign a Release of Information form
    d. Document the consultation

14. In a school setting, an MFT is working individually with a number of children who have been identified as "at-risk" for various reasons. In one session, a 12-year-old girl tells the therapist that the girl has been in 10 fights so far this school year, and shows off several scars she says are from the fights. The girl takes pride in her scars, saying, "This is how you prove you're tough." The MFT knows from school administration that physical confrontations among students are common at the school. The MFT should:

    a. Ask to photograph the student's scars as evidence that could be turned over to the school or police.
    b. Report suspected physical abuse to the MFT's local child protective service agency.
    c. Maintain confidentiality.
    d. Attempt to determine the ages of the students with whom the client has been fighting.

15. In preparation for a move to a new city, an MFT is selling her home. The MFT's real estate agent shows the home to prospective buyers. In discussing one prospective buyer, the MFT comes to realize that the individual is a current client. The MFT's photos and personal effects have been removed from the home, but if the sale were to move forward with the client, the client would ultimately learn that they were buying the MFT's home. What should the MFT do?

    a. Terminate therapy with the client, as this would become necessary with the pending move anyway and allows the client to participate in the home buying process as they see fit

    b. Consider whether the client is an appropriate buyer for the home, considering their symptoms, their socioeconomic status, and the neighborhood the home is in

    c. Seek consultation

    d. Without revealing that the prospective buyer is a client, give the real estate agent guidance on how to most effectively communicate with that buyer, based on the MFT's knowledge of them

16. An MFT is meeting for the first time with a family seeking treatment for their 16-year-old son. The parents report that the son was recently suspended from school for smoking marijuana, and admitted that he had been regularly using marijuana for several months. The MFT asks to speak with the boy individually. When the parents leave the room, the 16-year-old says, "You seem nice, but this is a waste of time. You and I both know I'm only here because my parents are making me come. I have no intention of stopping smoking. I'll just get better at hiding it from them." The MFT should:

    a. Report the 16-year-old's statements to the parents.

    b. Report the 16-year-old's ongoing criminal behavior to law enforcement.

    c. Inform the parents that the MFT cannot ethically conduct therapy as it is unlikely to be effective.

    d. Further assess the 16-year-old and his family.

17. An MFT receives a signed letter from a former client the MFT had discontinued treatment with six months earlier. The client had serious symptoms, and could not consistently attend therapy or afford the MFT's fee. The client owes the MFT more than $500. Now, the client is requesting a copy of their records so that the client can provide the records to their new therapist. The MFT should:

    a. Send the former client an invoice and let them know that they can obtain a copy of the file once the balance due has been paid

    b. Contact the client's new therapist to collaborate with them on diagnosis and treatment planning

    c. Provide the client with a copy of the treatment record

    d. Directly provide the new therapist with a copy of the treatment record, as the client may not pass along the full file to the new therapist

18. An MFT receives a referral from a psychiatrist. The client tells the MFT that she meets regularly with the psychiatrist to manage psychotic symptoms. After the client's initial session, she calls the MFT and sounds disoriented. She blames a recent medication change. The MFT is concerned and wants to discuss this with the psychiatrist, but the client has not signed a release of information. Considering the MFT's obligations under HIPAA, the MFT should:

    a. Understand that the client is in crisis and refer for an immediate medication monitoring appointment with the psychiatrist.

    b. Inquire as to possible extrapyramidal symptoms of the medication, and suggest the client stop taking the medication if necessary.

    c. Mail the client a Release of Information form and ask the client to bring it with them to the next session.

    d. Contact the psychiatrist to discuss the client's diagnosis and treatment planning.

19. Your new 34-year-old client recently moved to the US from Cuba. Though you are not familiar with Cuban culture, you find yourself strongly liking the client. She is intelligent and confident, and tells you that she is interested in becoming a therapist herself someday. You find it difficult to develop concrete therapeutic goals with her, as it seems the conversation in therapy over the first two sessions has been more social in nature. You should:

    a. Learn more about Cuban culture and social norms, to determine whether her behavior is normal.

    b. Because the client is from a culture that is not familiar to you, refer her to another therapist as she is outside your scope of competence.

    c. Attend therapy to address the pathology that underlies your immediate fondness for the client.

    d. Assign the treatment goals you feel would be best, reminding the client that she is free to participate or not participate in therapy as she sees fit.

20. A client has cancelled three of the last seven scheduled sessions with an MFT, and been a no-show for the other four. Each time, the client has promised to pay any balance charged, and to come in for a session the following week. The MFT finds herself irritated with the client's behavior, going so far as to warn the client two weeks ago that she would simply close the client's case and refer out if the client didn't come in. The client was a no-show for the next two scheduled sessions. Even before this long series of missed appointments, the MFT found herself personally disliking the client. How should the MFT manage her ethical responsibilities in this case?

    a. Meaningfully assess for crisis, and continue as the client's treatment provider if necessary.

    b. Close the case, providing the client with appropriate referrals to other providers.

    c. Provide the client at least two additional warnings, one of which must be in writing, prior to terminating therapy.

    d. Seek consultation to address countertransference, and continue to work toward the client more regularly attending therapy.

21. Your client is suing her employer, saying that long hours and stressful working conditions caused her anxiety disorder. You receive a subpoena from the employer's attorney, calling on you to produce the client's records and to testify in the case. You contact your client, who asks you not to testify or share her records. You should:

    a.   Advise her to drop or settle her lawsuit, since you will likely be required to testify and to share her records.
    b.   Respond to the subpoena by asserting privilege.
    c.   Waive privilege on the client's behalf, since an exception to privilege applies.
    d.   Provide no response to the subpoena, since it did not come from a judge.

22. An MFT wishes to advertise that the services she provides in her private practice. Which of the following would be an appropriate way for her to advertise her services?

    a.   "Rates as low as $35 per session."
    b.   "You will have a better life *and* a fatter wallet."
    c.   "The most effective therapy available."
    d.   "Pick up the phone and call now!"

23. A 13-year-old seeks mental health treatment at a nonprofit community clinic and is assigned to an Associate MFT. The Associate attempts to engage the 13-year-old in an assessment interview, and while she is not argumentative, the 13-year-old appears easily overwhelmed by the Associate MFT's questions and says very little. When the Associate MFT asks the 13-year-old whether she would like the Associate MFT to call her parents to pick her up, she simply shakes her head "no." When the Associate MFT asks the 13-year-old whether she understands what therapy is, she shrugs her shoulders. When the Associate asks whether the 13-year-old wants to keep taking with the Associate next week, she shakes her head "yes." Legally, the MFT should:

   a.   Schedule a session with the 13-year-old for the following week
   b.   Send a billing statement to the child's parents
   c.   Ask the 13-year-old to bring her parents to the next session, so that they can provide consent for treatment
   d.   Refer the client to a licensed MFT

24. An MFT is taking over another therapist's case on a short-term basis as the MFT is a leading expert in the family's presenting problem. The MFT asks whether the family would agree to allowing several newer therapists to observe the MFT's sessions from behind a one-way mirror. The family is initially hesitant, but says that they are willing if they can meet the observers after the observation is complete. The MFT should:

   a.   Document the conversation in progress notes and arrange for the family to meet the observers after observation.
   b.   Ask the family to provide consent for observation in writing.
   c.   Refuse the family's request to meet the observers and ask whether they would still be willing to allow the observation to occur.
   d.   Reduce the fee for observed sessions in exchange for allowing the observation to occur.

25. A 45-year-old person and their neighbor are opponents in a civil lawsuit about the boundary between their properties. The fight has gotten ugly, with each side accusing the other of harassment, vandalism, and mental illness. The person seeks out an MFT and asks whether the MFT can provide assessment of the person's personality and behavior to be used within the court process. The person denies any mental illness or any other symptoms or concerns for which they would want counseling. How should the MFT address their legal responsibilities?

    a. Refer the person to a psychologist
    b. Provide testing within the bounds of the 1984 Attorney General opinion, and submit a report to the court upon the person's request and authorization
    c. Require the person enter into a counseling process as a condition of providing the testing
    d. Provide testing and inform the court of the limitations of the MFT's role

26. A client who was dissatisfied with her therapy files a lawsuit against her former therapist, an MFT, accusing the MFT of failing to live up to professional standards. However, the client does not want her records to be released as part of the legal process, as she is concerned about others learning that she was diagnosed with a substance use disorder. Legally, the MFT:

    a. Will likely need to file a counterclaim against the client in order to have the records admitted in court.
    b. Is bound by a client's request to redact part of the file, such as the diagnosis, prior to the file being released.
    c. Will likely be able to have the client's records considered as part of the case.
    d. Cannot respond to the lawsuit, even to acknowledge that the person was a client, until she waives privilege.

27. A new client presents with symptoms including frequent crying spells, insomnia, hopelessness, weight gain, anhedonia, and thoughts of suicide. The client is different from the LMFT assessing him in many ways, including age, marital status, parental status (the client has two children, the LMFT has none) and even hobbies (the client is involved in sports, while the therapist enjoys knitting). How should the LMFT proceed?

   a. Refer the client out based on their demographic differences
   b. Recognize the limitations of their scope of competence and seek out training related to parents, married clients, and the role of sports in mental health
   c. No action is called for; proceed with assessment and treatment
   d. Review and discuss the clinical implications of all known differences

28. After several months of therapy, a client and their MFT decide together that treatment has been successful and it is time to move toward termination. They have a couple of sessions focused on carrying the client's gains forward. At what was supposed to be the final session, the client expresses hesitation, and says that they would rather keep coming to therapy indefinitely. How can the MFT best manage their ethical responsibility in this case?

   a. Agree to a limited number of additional sessions, and amend the treatment plan
   b. Gradually increase the client's fee as a behavioral nudge toward termination
   c. Agree to continue therapy indefinitely, as long as the client wants it
   d. Assess whether there is any potential benefit to additional sessions, and if not, proceed with termination

29. An MFT is struggling with what they perceive to be unfair treatment by agency administrators. They have had multiple meetings with the MFT to document her steadily declining clinical outcomes and productivity, and concerns about "erratic behavior" raised by coworkers. The MFT acknowledges that they have always been eccentric, but says that clients seem to appreciate and relate to this. The MFT is unaware of other clinicians at the agency being called in for similar meetings. In a recent session, the MFT said to a client, "I don't know why you keep coming here. The people who run this place are awful." How should the MFT proceed?

   a. Seek out treatment for the issues interfering with her work
   b. Seek out an attorney to address potential labor law violations by the employer
   c. Provide clients with information about other community agencies where they can seek help
   d. Document the meetings with administrators and share her concerns with her clinical supervisor

30. An MFT is working with a client in a different part of the state, one the MFT has never visited, via telemedicine. During a session taking place via videoconference, the client informs the therapist that he recently lost his job and is struggling to navigate the complex web of social services in his area. He fears losing his home in a matter of weeks. Ethically, the MFT should:

   a. Volunteer to serve as the client's case manager to better coordinate his services.
   b. Travel to where the client is located to provide services in person on a temporary basis.
   c. Reconsider whether telemedicine services are appropriate for this client.
   d. Assess for suicidality and substance use.

31. A client family has been struggling with financial needs since the father was furloughed from her job at a car wash. The family is in therapy to address areas of acculturation and family conflict. There are four boys in the family, ranging in ages from 3 to 13. While all of the family members sometimes come to therapy in dirty, torn clothes, the 8-year-old boy seems particularly withdrawn. He appears underweight, and says that the family sometimes waits for him to go to sleep before they eat dinner. "That's not right," the mother protests. "We send you to bed without dinner when you disobey." The mother expresses her frustration that the 8-year-old is frequently sick and needs to stay home from school. To resolve the MFT's legal obligations, the MFT should:

    a. Understand the impact of poverty and possible acculturation trauma
    b. Assess the family for violence
    c. Report suspected child neglect
    d. Ask the mother to provide a release allowing the MFT to review the 8-year-old's medical file

32. After several sessions of individual therapy focused on anger management, a client becomes visibly angry at his therapist. "I thought you knew what you were doing," the client says. "You misled me." The client pulls a brochure from his pocket and slams it on the table. It's a brochure the MFT is using to advertise his practice, and it describes the MFT as providing psychotherapy focused on anger and resentment issues. It also includes recommendations from two colleagues. Legally, the MFT should:

    a. Consider whether the client might have reasonably believed the MFT has more training or experience in anger management than he does
    b. Revise the brochure to remove the testimonials
    c. Revise the brochure to remove the word "psychotherapy"
    d. Consider termination

33. An Hispanic family approaches an MFT for family-based treatment. The MFT soon learns that several family members have their own individual therapists, and the parents in the family have a couple therapist who is working with them on their relationship. The family insists that these efforts are all in support of one another, and the family therapy would be to address family conflict and rule-setting. The family offers to pay the MFT the full fee, and insists they would attend every scheduled session. The MFT should:

    a. Inform the family that family therapy cannot take place until after the individual and couple therapy processes have concluded

    b. Inform the family that family therapy would be best conducted by the couple therapist, as that therapist is already familiar with the parents and can support them effectively in their parenting

    c. Require that the family sign releases allowing for contact with the other therapists, and proceed with family therapy only if all other therapists involved agree

    d. Ask the family to sign releases allowing for consultation and coordination with the other therapists, and proceed with family therapy

34. An MFT returns to work several weeks after a severe knee injury. She finds it difficult to focus during sessions because of the amount of pain she is experiencing, and does not remember much of each session after it has concluded. She finds her pain level increasing during the day. The MFT should:

    a. Assume this is part of the recovery process, and function as best as she can until the pain subsides.

    b. Consult with other MFTs who have dealt with physical injuries.

    c. Discontinue seeing clients until the pain is more manageable, making appropriate arrangements for continuity of care.

    d. Consult with her physician, and ask clients to sign a waiver stating that they understand she is dealing with an injury.

35. In group supervision, several MFT associates and their supervisor (who is a licensed MFT) are discussing whether the client of one of the associates should make a report of suspected child abuse. The associate who has seen the client says she does not believe the situation warrants a report. The other associates believe there is enough information to form reasonable suspicion of abuse, based on what the associate who has seen the client has said in describing the case. The supervisor validates the arguments being made by both sides, and after a long discussion, their positions are unchanged. The Associate MFT who has seen the case should:

    a. Make a report of suspected child abuse.
    b. Defer a decision on reporting until she can conduct further assessment.
    c. Hold to her belief that a report is not warranted unless new information comes to light that would change her view.
    d. Consult with the local child protective service agency.

36. An individual client tells an MFT that she is in fear of her husband. The couple has a long history of severe intimate partner violence, and there are protective orders in place requiring that they couple stay away from each other except when meeting in supervised locations to hand off their children. Now that the couple is finally divorcing, the husband has begun leaving threatening voicemails. The client plays one such voicemail for the MFT, who agrees that the client may be in danger. The MFT should:

    a. Notify law enforcement and warn the victim.
    b. Attempt to contact the husband to reduce the danger.
    c. Encourage the client to notify law enforcement.
    d. Notify the court that the husband is violating the protective order.

37. An MFT has received written permission from a former client family to use video of their sessions in group supervision. The MFT is interested in using segments from the videos as part of a workshop at an upcoming therapy conference. The MFT wonders whether the previous permission would apply to the conference setting, but is unable to reach the family, as the family has moved out of state. Ethically, the MFT should:

a. Only use the video segments at the conference if the MFT obtains specific written permission from the clients.

b. Only use the video segments at the conference if the MFT edits the videos such that none of the clients use any client names during the segments shown.

c. Only use the video segments at the conference if the MFT obtains written declarations from each workshop attendee that they will keep the contents of the workshop confidential.

d. Only use the video segments at the conference if the number of attendees at the workshop is comparable to the typical number of attendees in group supervision.

38. An MFT is brought in as an expert witness in a criminal case where a woman was accused of violently beating her 8-year-old daughter. The MFT is asked by the court to speak on the long-term effects of child abuse, as well as on factors that can lead mothers to become abusive. The MFT has expertise in these areas. The MFT also finds the behavior that the woman is accused of repugnant. The MFT should:

a. Speak solely about what the MFT knows about the specific case being tried, and avoid speaking in generalities.

b. Speak solely from her knowledge and expertise in the field, and avoid saying anything about the specific case being tried.

c. Clarify for the court that no explanatory factors for abuse should be understood as making child abuse acceptable.

d. Investigate the merits of the case before determining how to testify.

39. An MFT is doing an intake session with an individual client who begins discussing her family life. The MFT realizes that the client's spouse is someone the MFT had dated 10 years ago. The MFT remembers that relationship fondly, and is pleased to learn that the person the MFT had dated went on to get married. Ethically, the MFT should:

    a. Immediately disclose the MFT's realization and discuss with the client how they should proceed.

    b. Inform the client that the MFT cannot work with this client, and provide appropriate referrals.

    c. Evaluate whether the length of time since the relationship and the current fondness toward the client's spouse are sufficient to ensure that the therapy with this client would not be impacted.

    d. No action is called for.

40. The client of an MFT has been engaged in a difficult custody battle over her two sons. The client has shown the MFT photos, emails and text messages her husband has sent her, where he regularly talks about being drunk and often appears intoxicated. Though the children are all healthy, the client expresses fear for her children's safety around the father, and asks the MFT to inform the court that her husband may have a substance use disorder. The MFT should:

    a. Consider whether a report of child neglect is appropriate.

    b. Refuse to review these photos, emails, and text messages in the future, focusing instead on the client's reaction to them.

    c. Provide the court with a letter stating that, based on the limited information available, the MFT believes the husband may have a substance use disorder and should be further assessed.

    d. Refuse the client's request.

41. The client of an MFT comes to therapy with a wide smile, eager to tell the MFT what happened over the weekend. The client, who is 57, took her mother, who suffers from dementia, to see the Grand Canyon for the first time as a surprise birthday gift. The client reports that the mother angrily protested at first, not understanding why she was leaving her room at her nursing home. Once in the car, the client reports that her mother did not understand where they were going. But when her mother saw the Grand Canyon, the client reported "she was speechless. She was in awe." The MFT should:

    a. Report suspected elder abuse to the local adult protective services agency

    b. Direct the conversation back to issues relevant to the client's treatment

    c. Assess for potential elder abuse

    d. Ask the client to sign a Release of Information allowing the MFT to contact the mother and check on her current condition

42. A client has seen his MFT twice in the therapist's office. Before the third session, the client calls the MFT as the client is running late. The client asks whether the start of the session can be conducted via phone, with the understanding that he will arrive at the office about 20 minutes after the scheduled starting time. The MFT should:

    a. Inform the client that the session can begin when he arrives at the office

    b. Inform the clients of the risks and benefits of engaging in telehealth, and seek the client's consent for this form of treatment

    c. Conduct the initial 20 minutes of the session by phone

    d. Inform the client that while a phone session is prohibited, it would be possible to meet via real-time, two-way videoconferencing, either for the first 20 minutes or for the full session

43. An MFT who identifies as gay is working in an agency setting, and conducting an initial assessment session with a client who also identifies as gay. The client tells the MFT that he feels very trusting toward the MFT because they are both part of the LGBTQ community, so "I know you understand what I've gone through." The client becomes tearful at several points in the assessment, and on other occasions, the MFT believes the client is actively flirting with him. The MFT should:

    a. Provide the client a copy of the brochure *Therapy Never Includes Sexual Behavior*

    b. Transfer the client to a different therapist within the agency

    c. Understand the client behavior as part of the clinical picture and inquire about trauma history

    d. Consult with a colleague to minimize countertransference and ensure the MFT can maintain proper boundaries

44. An MFT takes notes during sessions in order to track key moments in session and important words or phrases used by various clients. The MFT keeps these handwritten notes separate from clients' files. The MFT receives a court order for all available treatment records on one of the MFT's clients. That client has an extensive file, as the MFT had seen the client for more than 100 sessions. The MFT should:

    a. Respond to the court order by asserting privilege.

    b. Respond to the court order by providing a treatment summary.

    c. Respond to the court order by providing the full file for the client, without the handwritten notes that had been kept separately.

    d. Respond to the court order by providing the full file for the client and all handwritten notes pertaining to the client's sessions.

45. An MFT is working with a religious family whose son has been diagnosed with a blood disorder. While not fatal, the disorder could significantly impact the boy's growth and development. The family tells you that after meeting with multiple doctors, they have elected to use only spiritual healing for their son, and to put his health "in God's hands." The MFT should:

    a. Advise the clients to utilize Western medicine techniques known to treat the disorder.
    b. Report suspected child abuse.
    c. Report suspected child neglect.
    d. Discuss with the family how they reached their decision and what its possible impacts could be.

46. An MFT has been working with a family to improve the parents' skills in managing their daughters' behavior. The family experiences frequent crises, and the MFT considers it her most difficult case. On the day before the MFT is scheduled to leave for a two-week vacation out of state, one of the daughters in the family admits to frequent drug use and self-injury. The parents call the MFT in a panic and ask for an emergency session. The MFT assesses the family by phone and determines that no one in the family is immediately suicidal or homicidal, though the parents are concerned that the daughter may become suicidal. The MFT should:

    a. Cancel or delay the planned vacation and attend to the urgent needs of the family.
    b. Plan on conducting at least occasional phone check-ins while she is on vacation to ensure family stability.
    c. Work with the family to arrange for a colleague to fill in for the MFT while on vacation, assessing the family and carrying the treatment plan forward.
    d. Report suspected child neglect based on the daughter's drug use and self-injury, which the family has not adequately protected her from.

47. An MFT has been seeing an individual client for three months. The client is struggling with post-traumatic stress following a military deployment. While the client is in therapy, the MFT gets to know the client's spouse, as the client signs a Release of Information allowing the MFT and the spouse to share information about the client's symptoms, treatment, and billing. Three months into the therapy, the MFT and the client's spouse encounter each other at a bar. They have sex that night. Legally, the MFT must now:

    a. Terminate the sexual relationship immediately, terminate the client relationship immediately, and self-report to the BBS

    b. Terminate the sexual relationship immediately, and immediately disclose the encounter to the client

    c. Terminate the sexual relationship immediately, encourage the client's spouse to disclose the encounter to the client, and provide the client a copy of the brochure *Therapy Never Includes Sexual Behavior*

    d. Take steps to minimize the emotional harm that may come to the client as a result of the encounter

48. A week after a particularly difficult session, a client arrives on time for her session with an MFT in the early afternoon. She brings a sandwich for the MFT, and offers it at the beginning of the session. She also pulls out a sandwich for herself, and asks whether it is OK for them both to eat during session. The MFT should:

    a. Politely refuse the offer and consider moving the client's sessions to a different time of day.

    b. Accept the sandwich and conduct the session over lunch, supporting the client's autonomy.

    c. Refuse the gift, but allow the client to have lunch in session to provide her with a sense of comfort and safety.

    d. Consider and discuss the larger ramifications for therapy.

49. A client asks to use her insurance to pay for therapy with an MFT, as she would not be able to pay out of pocket. The client's husband works for a large multinational corporation, and the client's insurance is provided through that corporation. The client tells the MFT that she believes she may have Borderline Personality Disorder and Substance Use Disorder, and does not want her husband or the corporation to learn of any diagnoses the MFT might give her. The MFT should:

    a. Provide referrals to low-fee clinics.

    b. Discuss what information is provided to insurers, and what the client's treatment options may be.

    c. Contact the insurer to advocate for the client.

    d. Advise the client to seek a court order that will seal her treatment records.

50. An MFT encounters a former client from many years ago at a party. They enjoy catching up socially, and are each impressed with the other. In the time since therapy, the former client has been married and divorced. The MFT, also now divorced, finds herself seeing the former client as an equal. She also finds herself attracted to the former client. Ethically, the MFT should:

    a. Provide the former client with a copy of the brochure *Therapy Never Includes Sexual Behavior*.

    b. Assess whether the former client also sees the MFT as an equal, and if so, consider initiating a romantic relationship.

    c. Review the reasons why the client sought therapy years ago, and determine whether the former client has truly resolved those concerns.

    d. Limit her social contact with the former client.

51. An MFT has been working with a family for several sessions and plans a session where the entire family will participate in a ceremony relieving the oldest daughter of the responsibility she has taken on as a co-parent. Shortly before the session, the mother informs the MFT that she will be away on a business trip and asks whether she can participate in the session by phone or videoconferencing. The mother's frequent absences are part of the reason why the daughter felt obligated to take on parenting tasks. The MFT should:

    a.   Contact the BBS to see whether the MFT can include the mother in session while she is on her trip.

    b.   Include the mother in the session and in the ceremony via phone or videoconference, and clarify that her involvement is consultation rather than therapy.

    c.   Refuse the mother's request and reschedule the ceremony for a time she can attend in person.

    d.   Contact the other family members to see whether they believe including the mother would be appropriate.

52. In an effort to address systemic racism and oppression in US society, an MFT decides to create three slots in her weekly schedule that she will use to provide no-fee therapy to African-American clients. She announces this with a flyer in her office. A Latino client asks whether he would also be eligible for one of those slots. The MFT should:

    a.   Ask the Latino client to demonstrate how the oppression he has experienced is comparable to that of African-Americans

    b.   Immediately agree to make the slot available to the Latino client as well, clarifying that it is open to all those who identify as people of color

    c.   Expand eligibility for these slots to include anyone who has experienced systemic oppression

    d.   Clarify that because of African-Americans' unique position in US society, these slots are only open to those who classify themselves as African-American

53. An MFT and their client disagree about how the client should handle an upcoming family reunion. The client has a history of problematic alcohol use leading to hospitalization. The MFT is concerned that the large amounts of alcohol likely to be served at the reunion could be triggering for the client, perhaps even leading to a relapse. The client is confident in their sobriety, and interested in seeing family members for the purposes of addressing past conflict. The MFT should:

    a. Argue strongly in support of the client not attending the reunion, while empathizing with the client's desire to attend and clarifying that it is the client's choice to make

    b. Considering the level of risk involved, make it a condition of continuing treatment that the client not attend the reunion

    c. Inquire about the client's reasons for wanting to attend the reunion in the presence of these risks

    d. Understand that the decision of whether to attend is the client's alone to make, and therefore do not raise the MFT's concerns in session

54. An MFT becomes seriously ill and is hospitalized, with the expectation that the hospitalization will be long-term. The MFT is suffering serious pain and difficulty with cognition due to the combination of medications the MFT is being given. The MFT has an active caseload of about 20 clients, some of whom are at risk for going into crisis and require regular contact. Under the circumstances, the MFT should:

    a. Conduct telehealth sessions from the MFT's hospital room until clients can be transferred

    b. Sell the MFT's practice, including its current active caseload, and inform clients in writing that as of the sale date, they will be attending sessions with the new practice owner

    c. Authorize another qualified clinician to access client records and coordinate continuity of care

    d. Send a letter to each client releasing them from the MFT's care and closing their cases

55. An MFT is treating an adolescent client who was mandated to therapy by the juvenile court system following a series of convictions for shoplifting, truancy, and other low-level offenses. The MFT has been treating the adolescent for six sessions with moderate progress when the client provides the MFT with a form from the court that the MFT is supposed to complete in order to evaluate the client's participation and progress in therapy. The form specifically asks the MFT to evaluate the client's preparedness to be released from probation. The form says it is to be returned by the MFT to the juvenile probation office. The MFT should:

    a.   Decline to complete the form
    b.   Complete those sections of the form that relate to dates of service and topics of therapy, while leaving evaluative questions blank
    c.   Complete the form and return it to the client to submit to the juvenile probation office
    d.   Complete the form and return it to the juvenile probation office as instructed

56. A client comes to an MFT and identifies herself as the victim of intimate partner violence. She describes instances of her husband physically assaulting her and threatening her with a gun. She tells the MFT that her husband is a police officer who is skilled with technology and monitors their bank accounts closely. She asks the MFT to see her on a cash-only basis with no physical receipts, and to not keep any records of her treatment, as she is worried those records could be used by her husband to discover where she is currently staying and to describe her in future divorce proceedings as mentally unfit for custody of their children. Considering the MFT's ethical responsibilities, the MFT should:

    a.   Agree to the client's requests
    b.   Agree to the client's requests surrounding payment, and inform her that clinical records must be kept, but that those records will not include any information about her mental health
    c.   Agree to the client's requests surrounding payment, and inform the client that records from treatment of intimate partner violence are not subject to subpoena
    d.   Inform the client that neither of her requests can be honored

57. A young adult seeks the services of an MFT to help him determine his life path. He specifically asks the MFT to help him learn how to perform household tasks like laundry and help with financial management, explaining that since he had spent many years in a series of foster homes as a child, he never learned these skills. The MFT should:

    a. Turn away the client and refer him to community resources.
    b. Turn away the client and refer him to three other therapists.
    c. Accept the client and focus on the skills he is asking to learn.
    d. Accept the client and focus on the trauma he suffered in the foster care system.

58. An Associate MFT is working for an LMFT in private practice. The Associate is interested in practicing via telehealth at some point in the future, and has a number of questions about applicable laws and regulations. The supervisor is not familiar with the current legal rules surrounding telehealth care. Ethically, the supervisor should:

    a. Direct the supervisee to research their specific questions, and report back to the supervisor on what they find
    b. Discontinue the supervision relationship and refer the associate to a supervisor who practices via telehealth
    c. Seek out a training course on current state laws and regulations for telehealth care, and inform the associate of what they learned in the course
    d. Inform the supervisee in writing that it is the supervisee's sole responsibility to ensure legal compliance with telehealth rules

59. A client who has expressed great concern about anyone knowing she is in therapy passes out in the middle of a session. The MFT the client was seeing is able to wake her long enough to learn that she has recently been struggling with illness and has pain from a neck injury, and the MFT knows from the client's intake paperwork that she has a blood disorder. The MFT should:

    a.   Stay with the client and continue attempting to wake her.
    b.   Call 911 and transport the client outside of the office into a public area to protect her privacy.
    c.   Call 911 and summon paramedics without providing any information about the client or her illness.
    d.   Call 911, summon paramedics, and inform them of the client's medical issues.

60. A couple has been attending therapy for four months with an MFT when they report a recent instance of relationship violence. One partner was left with several scratches and bruises, some of which are visible to the MFT. The other partner, who works as a school administrator, reports also having been injured. The couple largely agrees about what happened, and reports that this event has solidified their commitment to therapy. They have two children, but the children have been staying with their grandparents for the past several days, since before the violent event occurred. In considering the MFT's legal and ethical obligations, the MFT should:

    a.   Further assess the couple's immediate risk
    b.   Discontinue couple therapy and proceed with individual sessions
    c.   Because one partner is a school employee, the violence must be reported to law enforcement
    d.   Report suspected emotional abuse to a local child protective service agency

61. A woman who is seeing an MFT for treatment of depression dies under mysterious circumstances. In therapy, she had discussed her recreational drug use, and her fear that her ex-husband may become violent with her. The MFT receives a notice from the local coroner investigating the woman's cause of death that the coroner would like to review the woman's treatment records. The MFT should:

    a. Contact the woman's next of kin to determine their wishes

    b. Claim privilege on behalf of the client

    c. Offer to answer specific questions, but refuse to provide the treatment record

    d. Provide the requested records

62. A middle-aged man who is seeing a psychologist to work on his symptoms of anxiety inquires with an MFT about the possibility of the man and his wife seeing the MFT for couple counseling. The man explains that while some of his anxiety is about how others in his life perceive him, this is improving with treatment and he sees this as being markedly different from the work he and his wife would do with the MFT. The couple have been together for eight years and have two children. The MFT should:

    a. Defer the request and ask the man to wait for couple counseling until the individual treatment is concluded.

    b. Accept the man and his wife as a couple client, and encourage the man to discontinue individual therapy while the couple work is in progress.

    c. Consider the potential conflicts involved in the man seeing two therapists simultaneously for treatment of issues that may be intertwined.

    d. Refuse the request on the grounds that his anxiety is already being appropriately treated.

63. An MFT learns of a new cross-referral group on a popular social media site. The group is open to all health care professionals. To remain in the group, each person must agree to provide at least one referral a month to at least one other member of the group. A group administrator collects information about these referrals to ensure members are meeting the requirement. That information only includes the member making the referral, the members referred to, and the date, without any client information. The MFT believes joining this group will help build her practice. The MFT should:

    a.   Join the group and make referrals within it, as client confidentiality is protected.

    b.   Join the group and agree to the requirement, but explain to the group administrator that the MFT cannot provide any information on when referrals are made or to whom.

    c.   Join the group, make her commitment to her professional ethics known, and participate in the group in a manner most adherent to the ethics code possible given the group's requirements.

    d.   Not join the group as it runs counter to her legal responsibilities.

64. A wealthy client who is unfamiliar with therapy approaches an MFT and requests specific accommodations to protect the client's privacy. The client wants the MFT to meet with the client at the client's home for intensive, 3-hour sessions. The client wants the MFT to park on the street, and not in the client's driveway. The client wants the MFT to describe themselves as a florist to any photographers that may be outside the client's home. And the client wants to pay in cash, with no written records of the sessions. Ethically, the MFT should:

    a.   Refuse to lie to photographers or anyone else about their profession, but agree not to acknowledge that the client is in fact a client

    b.   Refuse to park on the street, as entering through the client's garage is more appropriate for preserving confidentiality

    c.   Refuse to agree not to maintain records, while expressing openness about the level of detail to be included in records

    d.   Refuse to engage in 3-hour sessions because of the possible intensity, and inform the client that therapy sessions cannot run longer than 90 minutes

65. An MFT with a full practice grows tired of working evenings, but recognizes that only evening times are convenient for many of the families she treats. She may:

    a. Take on two associates, and give ongoing clients with evening appointments to the associates.

    b. Express her frustration with evening sessions to her clients, and ask for their assistance in developing solutions.

    c. Discontinue accepting married couples or couples with children in her practice.

    d. With proper notice, add a $100 surcharge to appointments starting at 6pm or later.

66. An Associate MFT confides in her supervisor, a licensed MFT, that the associate has been having sexual fantasies about the supervisor. She expresses embarrassment about the fantasies and clarifies that she would never act on them, adding that she believes they stem from the supervisor helping her to feel safe as she learns how to be a therapist. The supervisor should:

    a. Further explore the reasons behind the fantasies to determine whether they would interfere with the supervisory process.

    b. Temporarily place the associate with a different supervisor until she is stabilized and able to be more present in supervision.

    c. Praise the associate's courage, direct her to her own therapist, and monitor the associate's behavior in supervision and with clients.

    d. Temporarily remove the associate from client care until further assessment can be completed and the fantasies can be addressed.

67. A client calls her therapist, an LMFT, from a train headed for Oregon. The LMFT is surprised to learn that the client is calling rather than attending in person, but as it is their scheduled session time, agrees to talk with the client by phone. The client tells the LMFT that she expects the train will cross into Oregon in about 20 minutes, but that there is no way for her to know when exactly that happens. The LMFT should:

    a. End the conversation within about 20 minutes.
    b. Continue the session for the fully scheduled time.
    c. Conduct a crisis assessment and then immediately end the call.
    d. Inquire as to the client's formal state of residency.

68. An LMFT has been working with a client who describes himself as a computer hacker. Sessions have focused on his difficulty in building friend-ships and romantic relationships. In session one day, the hacker tells the therapist that he was easily able to obtain a great deal of personal infor-mation about her, including her home address, bank account balances, and social security number. He sees that the LMFT is unsettled by this, and as-sures her he has no intention of misusing the information. The LMFT should:

    a. Contact law enforcement and report the data theft, without revealing that the person suspected is a client.
    b. Discontinue treatment and refer the client to at least three other therapists.
    c. Make it a condition of treatment that the client delete all of this data from any place where he has it stored.
    d. Consult with an attorney and monitor her accounts closely.

69. A new client expresses surprise when she comes to her first session with an MFT and finds that the MFT's dog is resting next to the MFT's chair. The client expresses discomfort with the animal's presence, as the client was bitten by a dog when she was a child. Legally, the MFT should:

   a. Provide the client with a letter establishing that the dog is an Emotional Support Animal
   b. Diagnose the client's phobia as a disability and remove the dog from the room immediately
   c. Challenge the client's cognitive distortions, and use the opportunity to provide safe exposure to a well-controlled animal
   d. Provide information on the MFT's fee structure prior to beginning treatment

70. A few days after a particularly difficult session, a client asks her therapist (an LMFT) to show her the information the LMFT wrote in the client's file about that session. The client had discussed childhood trauma and tells the LMFT she wants any information about that trauma removed immediately from the file. The LMFT empathizes with the client, but had included information about the trauma in progress notes and believes it is important to the client's treatment. Legally, the LMFT should:

   a. Comply with the client's request by sharing the progress note and removing any offending information from the file within 15 days.
   b. Inform the client that the client is free to review the file but that the LMFT cannot comply with the client's request to change the file.
   c. Inform the client that she may replace the progress note from the session with a statement of up to 250 words that she has written herself.
   d. Refuse the client's request and process her reasons for wanting to keep the information secret.

71. A couple has been seeing an LMFT for premarital counseling. Toward the end of the counseling, they ask the LMFT whether she would be willing to attend the wedding and speak briefly at the reception about what makes the couple such a good fit. They say they have no problem with introducing the LMFT honestly and describing her role, saying she has been very help-ful to them. They believe their families would be happy to meet her and to share their thanks as well. The LMFT should:

    a. Politely refuse the request.
    b. Consider the cultural implications of the request and the potential impact on any future treatment.
    c. Attend the wedding, but decline to speak, and ask that she not be introduced as a therapist.
    d. Have the clients sign a release of information authorizing the LMFT to speak candidly, and then do so, consistent with the clients' re-quest.

72. An adolescent male client tells an LMFT that he is drawn to violent mov-ies and video games, and spends a great deal of time fantasizing about what he would do if confronted with a situation where he would need to be-come violent to survive. Though he has no history of violence or substance use, the client is struggling in school and the family has guns in the home. The LMFT should:

    a. Assess for safety and for psychotic disorder.
    b. Assess for substance use disorder.
    c. Develop a safety plan.
    d. Engage in discussion of what makes the games, movies, and fanta-sies so appealing.

73. An Associate MFT has been working under supervision in a private practice setting for two years. The Associate achieves licensure, and informs the supervisor that the Associate will be starting their own private practice. The now-former Associate would like to bring their current clients along to the new practice. How can the Associate MFT best address their ethical responsibilities?

    a. Understand that the clients are ultimately clients of the supervisor, and allow the clients to determine how they wish to proceed.

    b. Understand that the clients are ultimately clients of the supervisor, and allow the supervisor to determine which clients may follow the new licensee into their private practice.

    c. Retain the files for all clients who wish to follow the new licensee into their private practice, allowing the supervisor to make copies if the supervisor wishes.

    d. Allow the clients to determine whether to follow the new licensee into private practice, paying the supervisor a fee for each client who does so. This fee covers the supervisor's costs for marketing that brought the clients in to see the Associate originally.

74. Your client has health insurance, but the insurance carrier is refusing to cover the client's therapy because she is seeing you for couple therapy and does not, in your assessment, qualify for a diagnosis of mental illness. You should:

    a. Assess the client's ability to advocate on her own behalf with the insurance company.

    b. Offer to include an "insurance diagnosis" on the client's paperwork to facilitate coverage.

    c. Work with the client to develop an alternative plan for payment.

    d. Discontinue therapy.

75. After consulting with an attorney and a colleague, an LMFT makes a child abuse report. The LMFT had learned from a family being seen together in treatment that the parents engage in physical punishment of their children. Three weeks after the report was made, the parents in the family ask directly in session whether the LMFT was the person who made the report. The parents have been frustrated and hope to confront the reporting party, as they do not believe their behavior is abusive and are embarrassed and angry that an investigator from the local child protective service agency visited their home and their child's school. The investigator was ultimately unable to substantiate the abuse report. Ethically, the LMFT should:

    a. Acknowledge having made the report and share the specific reasons why the LMFT did so.

    b. Acknowledge having made the report, apologize for having done so, and work to repair the relationship.

    c. Deny having made the report, and empathize with their emotional response to the investigation.

    d. Deny having made the report, and guide the conversation back to the reasons why the family is in treatment.

- STOP HERE -
END OF TEST

Quick Answer Key

Quick Answer Key

1. B	21. B	41. A	61. D
2. D	22. D	42. B	62. C
3. B	23. C	43. C	63. D
4. D	24. B	44. D	64. C
5. B	25. A	45. D	65. D
6. B	26. C	46. C	66. C
7. C	27. C	47. D	67. A
8. D	28. D	48. D	68. D
9. A	29. A	49. B	69. D
10. D	30. C	50. D	70. B
11. B	31. C	51. C	71. B
12. C	32. A	52. C	72. D
13. C	33. D	53. A	73. A
14. C	34. C	54. C	74. C
15. C	35. A	55. B	75. A
16. D	36. C	56. D	
17. C	37. A	57. A	
18. D	38. B	58. C	
19. A	39. B	59. D	
20. B	40. D	60. A	

Practice Test:
Answers and Rationales

1. An MFT refers a client to a local psychiatrist for an evaluation for possible medication treatment. A few weeks later, the MFT receives a card in the mail from the psychiatrist, saying "thank you for the kind referral" and including a $10 gift card for coffee. The client's name is not mentioned anywhere. How should the MFT manage their responsibilities?

    a. **Incorrect.** Thank the psychiatrist for the gift, also without mentioning any client names
    b. **CORRECT.** Return the gift
    c. **Incorrect.** Accept the gift if the MFT chooses, as it is for a trivial amount and no confidential information was inappropriately shared
    d. **Incorrect.** Forward the gift to the client rather than accepting it directly

It is against the law to give or receive kickbacks for referrals, so this gift must be refused (B). Accepting it (A or C) amounts to receiving a kickback for a referral; passing it along to the client (D) still means that the MFT accepted the gift.

2. A client comes to therapy expressing concern about his 94-year-old mother. The client tells the therapist that his mother, who lives a few houses down from the client, has been refusing to eat and is unwilling to leave her home to see a doctor. She is losing weight and appears to be in declining health, but wants simply to be left alone. The client is unsure of how to help. The MFT should:

   a. **Incorrect.** Encourage the client to openly discuss his concern with his mother. *An open discussion is unlikely to resolve the problem and does not address the MFT's responsibilities.*

   b. **Incorrect.** Encourage the client to transport his mother to a doctor for evaluation even if it means doing so against her will. *Transporting the mother to medical care against her will is questionable on a number of levels, and also does not address the MFT's reporting responsibility.*

   c. **Incorrect.** Encourage the client to report the situation to his local adult protective service agency. *Encouraging the son to report does have the advantage of the adult protective service agency being notified, but it would still represent a failure on the MFT's part to report in a mandated reporting situation.*

   d. **CORRECT.** Report the situation to the local adult protective service agency. *The mother's refusal to attend to basic needs (eating and medical care) and her apparent declining health suggest self-neglect. Even though the MFT did not learn about the problem directly from the elder, the MFT has enough information to reasonably suspect elder neglect. Reporting fulfills the MFT's obligation and may help the mother receive the services she needs.*

3. An MFT becomes nervous when her male client, who has been struggling with symptoms of psychosis, threatens to drive his car into oncoming traffic on the way home. If the therapist believes that the client poses a threat as the client leaves the office, the MFT should:

a. **Incorrect.** Determine from the client's file his address and most likely route home, so that possible victims on that route can be warned. *The possible victims are not reasonably identifiable, particularly since the therapist cannot definitively know what route the client will take home.*

b. **CORRECT.** Contact law enforcement to initiate the process of assessment for involuntary hospitalization. *The client poses an immediate danger, but the possible victims are not reasonably identifiable, particularly since the therapist cannot definitively know what route the client will take home. Therefore this is a situation calling for possible involuntary hospitalization, and not a* Tarasoff *situation.*

c. **Incorrect.** Contact law enforcement to have the client arrested. *As the client has not yet committed a crime, the therapist could not ask to have him arrested.*

d. **Incorrect.** Maintain confidentiality, as the client has not threatened any identifiable victims. *Action is called for, as much to protect the client as others; maintaining confidentiality leaves an immediately dangerous client on the roads.*

4. A couple living in a rural area seeks online treatment from an MFT in a large city more than 100 miles away. The MFT specializes in infidelity, and one partner recently revealed a six-month affair. The other partner has been deeply distressed, unable to sleep since that time. During an initial phone call, the couple tells the MFT that they do not have a computer of their own, and so will be using the computer and webcam at the home of one of their parents. The MFT informs the clients of the risks and benefits of online therapy, and the couple agrees to go forward. During the first session, the MFT notices that people – presumably the parents – are walking by in the background, and the couple often seems uncomfortable discussing their relationship. The session is cut short when the couple accidentally disconnects the microphone, and they cannot figure out how to get it working again. Though unable to hear them, the MFT observes the couple's frustration and disappointment. The MFT should:

a. **Incorrect.** Schedule an in-person consultation with the couple at the MFT's office. *Asking the couple to come all the way to the MFT's office may present an unreasonable burden to the clients.*

b. **Incorrect.** Ask the couple to ensure that no other people will be around when they are doing an online session. *Keeping other people out of the background during a session would be helpful but does not resolve the technology issues they couple is having.*

c. **Incorrect.** Remind the clients of the risks and benefits of online services. *Simply reminding them of risks and benefits does not resolve any of the problems that have arisen.*

d. **CORRECT.** Attempt to connect the clients with qualified providers of in-person services in their area. *One of the ethical requirements of MFTs is that we only use online services when they are clinically appropriate, considering the clients' needs and abilities. In this situation, their needs and abilities do not appear to match well with what the MFT can offer online.*

5. After a few sessions, a client tells an MFT that the client can no longer afford to pay for services. However, the client makes blankets and scarves at her home, bartering is common in her culture and neighborhood, and she would be willing to exchange these goods for sessions at fair market value. How should the MFT manage their ethical obligations?

    a. **Incorrect.** Work with the client on a pro bono basis. Inform the client that the MFT would happily accept a single scarf as a gift, to protect the therapeutic relationship, but that this would be separate from any payment for services

    b. **CORRECT.** Develop a clear contract with the client establishing the market value of the goods, when they are to be received, and how many sessions will be provided in exchange

    c. **Incorrect.** Terminate therapy for inability to pay, and provide referrals to community resources

    d. **Incorrect.** Allow the client to carry a balance for therapy, until such time as the client can sell enough blankets and scarves to pay for services

Therapists are encouraged, but not required, to provide pro bono services generally; we are never ethically required to provide pro bono services to a specific client (A). In that option, the scarf is framed as sort of a payment, but sort of not; it would likely be perceived as bartering but without the necessary contract to establish clarity. We also are not required to allow a client to build a significant balance (D), and doing so may even be considered exploitive when the client is unlikely to be able to pay in the foreseeable future. Termination (C) is an option, but not the best one here, as bartering is an option that continues treatment while preserving the integrity of the relationship. Bartering requires a clear contract, which (B) establishes.

6. An LMFT working in an agency setting learns that a child she sees for therapy has been physically abused by the child's parents. The parents are treated by another therapist at the same agency, and it was that therapist who shared the information about the abuse and is preparing a written report to the local child protective service agency. The LMFT believes she has information from her last meeting with the child that would be relevant to the abuse report. How should the LMFT proceed?

    a. **Incorrect.** File her own independent report of suspected child abuse, based on the information she learned from the colleague

    b. **CORRECT.** Provide the relevant information to the colleague, and collaborate on the report

    c. **Incorrect.** Take no action

    d. **Incorrect.** Because the LMFT is the victim's direct therapist, ask the colleague to provide all the available information and allow the LMFT to determine what will be reported

Assuming that the LMFT believes the information from the colleague is accurate, she has an obligation to ensure that a report is filed. As such, (C) is incorrect. However, in a treatment team setting, one provider can file a report on behalf of the team, and that (B) is what should happen here. An independent report (A) is not a violation of law, but nor would it be especially helpful, as it would largely rely on the LMFT's third-hand reporting. The LMFT is not in a position to independently determine what information will be shared (D), as the colleague is also a mandated reporter and needs to participate in reporting in some way.

7. A 59-year-old woman is living in a nursing home and struggling with early-onset dementia. Three of her daughters come to an MFT for family therapy to address their conflict surrounding their mother's treatment. In session, the two younger daughters say that the older daughter is refusing to let them see their mother, and does not even allow the mother to receive letters or phone calls. The older daughter acknowledges this, but says it is in everyone's best interests, as medical staff at the nursing home have informed her that the mother may not recognize her daughters. The older daughter says she is doing her best to spare everyone as much pain as she can. How should the MFT manage responsibilities in this case?

    a. **Incorrect.** Provide family therapy to address conflict among the daughters. Request a Release of Information that would allow the MFT to speak with nursing home staff and the mother, to see whether the mother may be able to participate in some way

    b. **Incorrect.** Ask the older daughter to verify her medical credentials that might allow her to make this determination for her family

    c. **CORRECT.** Report suspected dependent adult abuse to the local adult protective service agency

    d. **Incorrect.** Refer the family to an attorney to discuss power of attorney and related issues surrounding medical decision-making

While A, B, and D all may be *clinically* appropriate in certain circumstances, only C addresses a legal or ethical obligation – in this case, the legal obligation to report suspected dependent adult abuse. The older daughter's restrictions do not appear to have any medical basis; even by her report, the medical staff have only said that the mother may not recognize the daughters, not that seeing them would in some way be distressing or harmful. There is no rationale given for refusing letters or phone calls. This would be considered Isolation, which is a form of elder and dependent adult abuse.

8. After years of providing services in the office, an MFT decides to transition their practice to be exclusively online. The MFT selects a new videoconferencing platform that advertises itself as being secure and HIPAA-compliant. In a letter, the MFT informs all existing office clients that their care will be moved online as of roughly one month from the date of the letter. Prior to completing this transition, what must the MFT do to address their ethical responsibilities?

    a. **Incorrect.** Terminate or refer out all in-person clients with serious symptoms

    b. **Incorrect.** Allow the clients to choose whether they would like to continue seeing the MFT in-office rather than moving to telehealth

    c. **Incorrect.** Take reasonable steps to identify crisis resources local to each client

    d. **CORRECT.** Take a training on using the videoconference software

While not every client can be successfully treated via telehealth, there is no ethical or legal obligation to refer out on the basis of "serious symptoms" (A). Instead, the obligation is to assess whether each client is appropriate for telehealth. Some clients with serious symptoms (such as serious depression or agoraphobia) might even be particularly well-suited to telehealth. The MFT is not obligated to honor client preferences about in-person care (B); such an obligation would mean that a client could bind a therapist to their physical office for months or even years beyond when the therapist would want to leave that office. Identifying crisis resources (C) is a legal obligation, not an ethical one. Ethically, the MFT must ensure that they are adequately trained in the technology being used (D).

9. An MFT has been conducting telehealth sessions via video with a 23-year-old client. In the middle of a session, the client's boyfriend walks into the frame, visible to the therapist, kisses the client, and appears to leave their home to go to work. The MFT should:

a. **CORRECT.** Discuss the risks to confidentiality when working online
b. **Incorrect.** Ask the client to sign a Release of Information form allowing disclosure of therapeutic information, even if incidental, to the partner
c. **Incorrect.** Ask the partner to sign a Release of Information form allowing them to receive therapeutic information
d. **Incorrect.** Discontinue the session and, in writing, remind the client that therapy is to be conducted only from a private, confidential setting. If the client cannot find such a setting, they are inappropriate for telehealth

It is ultimately the responsibility of the client, and not the therapist, to control privacy and confidentiality at the client's end during technology-based sessions. In this instance, because any disclosure of information is being caused by the client and not the MFT, a Release of Information is not necessary, either from the client (B) or the partner (C). An MFT does, however, have an ethical obligation to remind clients of the limits of confidentiality where appropriate, as well as a responsibility to discuss with clients the risks associated with technology-based work. While suddenly discontinuing the session (D) would be an over-reaction – the partner is now gone, so there is no immediate risk of additional disclosures – it would be appropriate for the MFT to discuss the risks to confidentiality when working online (A).

10. An MFT is treating a middle-aged woman whose treatment is being paid for by the client's sister. The MFT has never met or spoken with the sister. The client simply brings in a check for each session, written by her sister and made payable to the therapist. After several weeks of treatment, the sister phones the therapist and asks what the payments were being used for. "I thought she was getting medical treatment, but now she's tells me she's been spending my money on this psychobabble nonsense," the sister says. The MFT should:

a. **Incorrect.** Argue that psychotherapy is a valid form of treatment, without discussing the client specifically. *Advocating for clients with third-party payers is worthwhile, but engaging in that argument here would provide at least implicit acknowledgement that the MFT is serving as the client's therapist. Without a release of information allowing the MFT to do so, that may be considered a breach of confidentiality.*

b. **Incorrect.** Provide limited information on the client, including service dates, diagnosis, and types of service, that the sister is legally entitled to as the payer. *Simply providing payment, particularly in the manner in which the sister is paying, does not entitle the payer to clinical information such as diagnosis.*

c. **Incorrect.** Offer to refund the sister's payments and collect fees directly from the client. *Immediately offering to refund the sister's payments and collect fees directly from the client suffers from the same confidentiality concern as option A above.*

d. **CORRECT.** Listen to the sister without offering any information on the client, and encourage the client to discuss the issue with her sister. *Listening without providing any information preserves the client's confidentiality and allows her to resolve the payment issues directly with her sister. It also may allow time for the client to sign a release of information, enabling the MFT have better advocate for the client with her sister.*

11. An MFT is planning her retirement in a few months, and has agreed to sell her private practice to a local colleague. Several weeks before she turns the practice over, the MFT should:

    a. **Incorrect.** Inform clients of her plans, and instruct them to continue as usual with the colleague as the colleague takes over. *Clients have autonomy in choosing their treatment provider. The therapist can make referrals, but cannot simply instruct clients to transfer to the new provider.*

    b. **CORRECT.** Inform clients of her plans, and request that each client who wishes to continue treatment with the colleague sign a Release of Information form allowing their files to be transferred. *While the office location may be the same, the clients who continue with the colleague are changing treatment providers. It makes good sense to formally allow the transfer of records and even to sign a new informed consent document with the colleague.*

    c. **Incorrect.** Inform clients of her plans, and offer to do a series of transitional sessions with each client while they are simultaneously starting therapy with the colleague. *Concurrent treatment can be problematic in several ways, and ethical codes discourage (but do not prohibit) it. A cleaner break would better support continuity in care.*

    d. **Incorrect.** Inform clients of her plans, and draft a transition document for the colleague. *It is not clear what such a document would or should entail.*

12. An MFT finds herself enjoying sessions with a high-functioning client who comes in to discuss her occasional anxiety symptoms. The MFT and client have similar tastes and similar senses of humor. The client asks whether the MFT might be interested in joining the client for lunch on a regular basis, separate from their therapy relationship. Ethically, the MFT should:

    a. **Incorrect.** Consider whether engaging in a friendship with the client would be detrimental to the therapy. *The MFT's consideration of possible detriment is irrelevant; the relationship is specifically prohibited regardless of the degree of detriment.*

    b. **Incorrect.** Inform the client that they could only engage in a friendship once two years have passed since the last professional contact. *While the "two-year rule" applies specifically to sexual relationships, the power differential between client and therapist is a consideration here as well.*

    c. **CORRECT.** Politely refuse the offer. *Close personal relationships are one of the forms of dual relationship specifically prohibited by professional ethical codes.*

    d. **Incorrect.** Join the client for lunch on a one-time basis, in support of the therapeutic relationship. *If the MFT joined the client for lunch on a one-time basis, it would at best be confusing to the client. Who would be expected to pay for the lunch? Could the client expect confidentiality if the MFT framed the lunch as being in support of the therapy? What if the client said things at lunch that the MFT would want to bring up in session? Better to keep the boundaries of the therapy relationship clearly defined.*

13. After an especially difficult session with a client an MFT considers to have a personality disorder, the MFT seeks to consult with a former professor from the MFT's graduate degree program, who is now retired. The MFT plans to call the professor to ask how the professor might handle the case, including asking about specific interventions and asking about whether the MFT should consider referring the case out. Legally, the MFT should:

    a. **Incorrect.** Share specific information about the session only if they are careful not to mention the client's name

    b. **Incorrect.** Establish a written contract with the professor for the consultation

    c. **CORRECT.** Ask the client to sign a Release of Information form

    d. **Incorrect.** Document the consultation

Establishing a written contract (B) and documenting the consultation (D) are both good ideas, but neither is legally required. Since the professor is not actively involved on the client's treatment team, the MFT cannot share information about the case without a release – even if the MFT withholds the client's name (A). The MFT should have the client sign a Release of Information prior to engaging in the consultation (C).

14. In a school setting, an MFT is working individually with a number of children who have been identified as "at-risk" for various reasons. In one session, a 12-year-old girl tells the therapist that the girl has been in 10 fights so far this school year, and shows off several scars she says are from the fights. The girl takes pride in her scars, saying, "This is how you prove you're tough." The MFT knows from school administration that physical confrontations among students are common at the school. The MFT should:

   a. **Incorrect.** Ask to photograph the student's scars as evidence that could be turned over to the school or police. *This inappropriately places the MFT in the role of an investigator.*
   b. **Incorrect.** Report suspected physical abuse to the MFT's local child protective service agency. *Physical abuse reporting standards include an exception for mutual fighting between minors of similar ages.*
   c. **CORRECT.** Maintain confidentiality. *No report is called for based on the information in the vignette.*
   d. **Incorrect.** Attempt to determine the ages of the students with whom the client has been fighting. *Unless the information would be sought for clinical reasons, pursuing this information places the MFT in the role of investigator of possible abuse.*

15. In preparation for a move to a new city, an MFT is selling her home. The MFT's real estate agent shows the home to prospective buyers. In discussing one prospective buyer, the MFT comes to realize that the individual is a current client. The MFT's photos and personal effects have been removed from the home, but if the sale were to move forward with the client, the client would ultimately learn that they were buying the MFT's home. What should the MFT do?

   a. **Incorrect.** Terminate therapy with the client, as this would become necessary with the pending move anyway and allows the client to participate in the home buying process as they see fit
   b. **Incorrect.** Consider whether the client is an appropriate buyer for the home, considering their symptoms, their socioeconomic status, and the neighborhood the home is in
   c. **CORRECT.** Seek consultation
   d. **Incorrect.** Without revealing that the prospective buyer is a client, give the real estate agent guidance on how to most effectively communicate with that buyer, based on the MFT's knowledge of them

This situation happens regularly in rural areas and more insular communities, and is not inherently problematic. In considering the MFT's obligations, they are obligated to assess the risks of this potential dual relationship, and to take steps to minimize risk accordingly. While selling one's home is likely not a "business relationship" as the CAMFT code of ethics would define it, terminating therapy prematurely to sell the home (A) is potentially exploitive. Using the MFT's therapeutic knowledge of the client to guide the real estate agent (D) or serve as a community gatekeeper (B) would be a misuse of the therapist's role, and also could be seen as exploitive (D) or potentially discriminatory (B). Only (C) here is an appropriate step for managing a potential dual relationship.

16. An MFT is meeting for the first time with a family seeking treatment for their 16-year-old son. The parents report that the son was recently suspended from school for smoking marijuana, and admitted that he had been regularly using marijuana for several months. The MFT asks to speak with the boy individually. When the parents leave the room, the 16-year-old says, "You seem nice, but this is a waste of time. You and I both know I'm only here because my parents are making me come. I have no intention of stopping smoking. I'll just get better at hiding it from them." The MFT should:

a.   **Incorrect.** Report the 16-year-old's statements to the parents. *Depending on how confidentiality has been arranged in this instance, the MFT may have the option of sharing this information with the parents. However, it is not clear that this is in anyone's best interest. In any case, the word "should" in the question suggests a focus on the MFT's obligations rather than their options. There is no obligation to share this information with parents.*

b.   **Incorrect.** Report the 16-year-old's ongoing criminal behavior to law enforcement. *His behavior does not qualify as an exception to confidentiality, so informing law enforcement would be a violation of confidentiality.*

c.   **Incorrect.** Inform the parents that the MFT cannot ethically conduct therapy as it is unlikely to be effective. *Resistance is common at the initial stages of therapy and should not be taken to mean that therapy cannot be effective. Further assessment is called for.*

d.   **CORRECT.** Further assess the 16-year-old and his family. *Resistance is common at the initial stages of therapy and should not be taken to mean that therapy cannot be effective. Further assessment is called for.*

17. An MFT receives a signed letter from a former client the MFT had discontinued treatment with six months earlier. The client had serious symptoms, and could not consistently attend therapy or afford the MFT's fee. The client owes the MFT more than $500. Now, the client is requesting a copy of their records so that the client can provide the records to their new therapist. The MFT should:

    a. **Incorrect.** Send the former client an invoice and let them know that they can obtain a copy of the file once the balance due has been paid

    b. **Incorrect.** Contact the client's new therapist to collaborate with them on diagnosis and treatment planning

    c. **CORRECT.** Provide the client with a copy of the treatment record

    d. **Incorrect.** Directly provide the new therapist with a copy of the treatment record, as the client may not pass along the full file to the new therapist

The MFT cannot deny access to treatment records simply because the client owes a balance (A). And the MFT has neither permission nor legal authority to communicate directly with the new therapist (B) and (D); while collaboration on treatment planning is allowed without a release, that only applies when _both_ providers are actively involved on the client's treatment team. The MFT should provide a copy of the record as per the former client's request (C).

18. An MFT receives a referral from a psychiatrist. The client tells the MFT that she meets regularly with the psychiatrist to manage psychotic symptoms. After the client's initial session, she calls the MFT and sounds disoriented. She blames a recent medication change. The MFT is concerned and wants to discuss this with the psychiatrist, but the client has not signed a release of information. Considering the MFT's obligations under HIPAA, the MFT should:

a. **Incorrect.** Understand that the client is in crisis and refer for an immediate medication monitoring appointment with the psychiatrist. *The client's disorientation may or may not be a crisis, and consultation with the psychiatrist is allowed under HIPAA (see option D below).*

b. **Incorrect.** Inquire as to possible extrapyramidal symptoms of the medication, and suggest the client stop taking the medication if necessary. *A suggestion to stop taking medication is medical advice and is outside of the MFT's scope of practice.*

c. **Incorrect.** Mail the client a Release of Information form and ask the client to bring it with them to the next session. *The client's disorientation may suggest a more urgent problem, one that can be resolved quickly without violating HIPAA. See option D below.*

d. **CORRECT.** Contact the psychiatrist to discuss the client's diagnosis and treatment planning. *HIPAA specifically allows two people who are both actively providing treatment to a client to communicate without a release for the purposes of diagnosis and treatment planning.*

19. Your new 34-year-old client recently moved to the US from Cuba. Though you are not familiar with Cuban culture, you find yourself strongly liking the client. She is intelligent and confident, and tells you that she is interested in becoming a therapist herself someday. You find it difficult to develop concrete therapeutic goals with her, as it seems the conversation in therapy over the first two sessions has been more social in nature. You should:

   a. **CORRECT.** Learn more about Cuban culture and social norms, to determine whether her behavior is normal.
   b. **Incorrect.** Because the client is from a culture that is not familiar to you, refer her to another therapist as she is outside your scope of competence.
   c. **Incorrect.** Attend therapy to address the pathology that underlies your immediate fondness for the client.
   d. **Incorrect.** Assign the treatment goals you feel would be best, reminding the client that she is free to participate or not participate in therapy as she sees fit.

This client offers you the opportunity to expand your scope of competence. Doing so will help you determine whether the social conversation in the first two sessions is a culturally accepted way of building trust and familiarity with a professional, or whether it is more troublesome. (B) is incorrect because this could be considered discrimination based on national origin. (C) is incorrect because it is not automatically pathological for you to like a client who is confident and intelligent. While you would want to remain aware of how your biases may be impacting treatment, simply liking a client does not require your own therapy. (D) is incorrect because it is not up to the therapist alone to determine the goals of treatment. Goals should be established collaboratively, and to do otherwise may violate a client's right to autonomy.

20. A client has cancelled three of the last seven scheduled sessions with an MFT, and been a no-show for the other four. Each time, the client has promised to pay any balance charged, and to come in for a session the following week. The MFT finds herself irritated with the client's behavior, going so far as to warn the client two weeks ago that she would simply close the client's case and refer out if the client didn't come in. The client was a no-show for the next two scheduled sessions. Even before this long series of missed appointments, the MFT found herself personally disliking the client. How should the MFT manage her ethical responsibilities in this case?

    a. **Incorrect.** Meaningfully assess for crisis, and continue as the client's treatment provider if necessary.
    b. **CORRECT.** Close the case, providing the client with appropriate referrals to other providers.
    c. **Incorrect.** Provide the client at least two additional warnings, one of which must be in writing, prior to terminating therapy.
    d. **Incorrect.** Seek consultation to address countertransference, and continue to work toward the client more regularly attending therapy.

You can terminate therapy for almost any reason, so long as that reason is not discriminatory in nature, any evident crisis issues are addressed, and the client is provided with appropriate referrals. In this case, the client has a pattern of non-attendance and was warned that this would lead to termination. There is no legal or ethical responsibility to provide redundant warnings ©. While assessing for crisis is generally a good idea (A), even if crisis issues were present, this would not necessarily obligate the therapist to remain the client's treatment provider. If anything, evidence of crisis combined with non-attendance in therapy might suggest a need for coordinated transfer to a higher level of care. While the MFT's response to the client may indeed indicate countertransference (D), therapists are not required to continue working with clients they don't like. Termination is appropriate here.

21. Your client is suing her employer, saying that long hours and stressful working conditions caused her anxiety disorder. You receive a subpoena from the employer's attorney, calling on you to produce the client's records and to testify in the case. You contact your client, who asks you not to testify or share her records. You should:

    a. **Incorrect.** Advise her to drop or settle her lawsuit, since you will likely be required to testify and to share her records.

    b. **CORRECT.** Respond to the subpoena by asserting privilege.

    c. **Incorrect.** Waive privilege on the client's behalf, since an exception to privilege applies.

    d. **Incorrect.** Provide no response to the subpoena, since it did not come from a judge.

The correct answer is B. While an exception to privilege does apply here, only the client or a judge can waive privilege. Until you know that either the client has waived privilege or a judge has determined that privilege does not apply, asserting privilege is a good default position. You also can get there by process of elimination: A is an incorrect response because giving the client legal advice would be outside of an MFT's scope of practice; C would be an incorrect response since it is never up to the therapist to determine whether privilege will be waived; and D is an incorrect response because failure to respond to a subpoena is not advisable.

22. An MFT wishes to advertise that the services she provides in her private practice. Which of the following would be an appropriate way for her to advertise her services?

    a.   **Incorrect.** "Rates as low as $35 per session." *State law requires advertising that includes prices to be specific, in order to avoid what is known as "bait and switch" advertising. This statement would violate the law.*

    b.   **Incorrect.** "You will have a better life *and* a fatter wallet." *This appears to present a guarantee to consumers. If "will" were replaced with "could," it would be more acceptable.*

    c.   **Incorrect.** "The most effective therapy available." *Any claims of effectiveness must be supported with peer-reviewed scientific studies. At present, there is not one single "most effective therapy available," as the effectiveness of therapies varies by problem type.*

    d.   **CORRECT.** "Pick up the phone and call now!" *This kind of call to action is not prohibited.*

23. A 13-year-old seeks mental health treatment at a nonprofit community clinic and is assigned to an Associate MFT. The Associate attempts to engage the 13-year-old in an assessment interview, and while she is not argumentative, the 13-year-old appears easily overwhelmed by the Associate MFT's questions and says very little. When the Associate MFT asks the 13-year-old whether she would like the Associate MFT to call her parents to pick her up, she simply shakes her head "no." When the Associate MFT asks the 13-year-old whether she understands what therapy is, she shrugs her shoulders. When the Associate asks whether the 13-year-old wants to keep taking with the Associate next week, she shakes her head "yes." Legally, the MFT should:

   a. **Incorrect.** Schedule a session with the 13-year-old for the following week

   b. **Incorrect.** Send a billing statement to the child's parents

   c. **CORRECT.** Ask the 13-year-old to bring her parents to the next session, so that they can provide consent for treatment

   d. **Incorrect.** Refer the client to a licensed MFT

Under state law, minors 12 and older can consent to treatment on their own – including with Associates – *so long as the minor is mature enough to participate intelligently in treatment.* This question focuses on that last part. There is not enough evidence here to suggest that she is, and ample evidence that she is not. As such, treatment should not proceed without parental consent ©. Proceeding without that consent (A) would be a violation of law. Parents cannot be billed for treatment for which they did not consent (B). Associates can treat minors consenting on their own (making D incorrect).

24. An MFT is taking over another therapist's case on a short-term basis as the MFT is a leading expert in the family's presenting problem. The MFT asks whether the family would agree to allowing several newer therapists to observe the MFT's sessions from behind a one-way mirror. The family is initially hesitant, but says that they are willing if they can meet the observers after the observation is complete. The MFT should:

   a. **Incorrect.** Document the conversation in progress notes and arrange for the family to meet the observers after observation. *MFTs are ethically required to obtain written permission for third-party observation.*

   b. **CORRECT.** Ask the family to provide consent for observation in writing. *MFTs are ethically required to obtain written permission for third-party observation. The family's request to meet the observers may be unusual, but could increase their comfort with being observed. Granting the request is empowering to the clients.*

   c. **Incorrect.** Refuse the family's request to meet the observers and ask whether they would still be willing to allow the observation to occur. *The family's request to meet the observers may be unusual, but could increase their comfort with being observed. Granting the request is empowering to the clients.*

   d. **Incorrect.** Reduce the fee for observed sessions in exchange for allowing the observation to occur. *This appears to be buying the family's permission to be observed. More importantly, it does not address the need for written permission for observation.*

25. A 45-year-old person and their neighbor are opponents in a civil lawsuit about the boundary between their properties. The fight has gotten ugly, with each side accusing the other of harassment, vandalism, and mental illness. The person seeks out an MFT and asks whether the MFT can provide assessment of the person's personality and behavior to be used within the court process. The person denies any mental illness or any other symptoms or concerns for which they would want counseling. How should the MFT address their legal responsibilities?

   a. **CORRECT.** Refer the person to a psychologist
   b. **Incorrect.** Provide testing within the bounds of the 1984 Attorney General opinion, and submit a report to the court upon the person's request and authorization
   c. **Incorrect.** Require the person enter into a counseling process as a condition of providing the testing
   d. **Incorrect.** Provide testing and inform the court of the limitations of the MFT's role

(B) here is not possible, as the 1984 AG opinion requires that MFTs only do testing with individuals with whom the MFT has a counseling relationship. You might then think it makes sense to establish that relationship (C), but the client expresses neither the need nor the desire for counseling, so forcing them into such a relationship is ethically problematic. Without such a relationship, the MFT cannot provide testing, even if they cautioned the court in their report (D). The only legally viable option presented here is (A).

26. A client who was dissatisfied with her therapy files a lawsuit against her former therapist, an MFT, accusing the MFT of failing to live up to professional standards. However, the client does not want her records to be released as part of the legal process, as she is concerned about others learning that she was diagnosed with a substance use disorder. Legally, the MFT:

    a.   **Incorrect.** Will likely need to file a counterclaim against the client in order to have the records admitted in court. *The determination of whether an exception to privilege applies does not require a counterclaim.*

    b.   **Incorrect.** Is bound by a client's request to redact part of the file, such as the diagnosis, prior to the file being released. *A specific exception to privilege applies here, and would likely mean that the full file could be released, though a determination of this would be up to a judge.*

    c.   **CORRECT.** Will likely be able to have the client's records considered as part of the case. *A specific exception to privilege applies when an MFT is sued and accused of failing to perform their role appropriately.*

    d.   **Incorrect.** Cannot respond to the lawsuit, even to acknowledge that the person was a client, until she waives privilege. *An MFT is entitled to defend themselves appropriately. A reasonable first step would be for the MFT to contact their attorney and have the attorney ask a court to determine that the client's records are not subject to privilege.*

27. A new client presents with symptoms including frequent crying spells, insomnia, hopelessness, weight gain, anhedonia, and thoughts of suicide. The client is different from the LMFT assessing him in many ways, including age, marital status, parental status (the client has two children, the LMFT has none) and even hobbies (the client is involved in sports, while the therapist enjoys knitting). How should the LMFT proceed?

    a. **Incorrect.** Refer the client out based on their demographic differences

    b. **Incorrect.** Recognize the limitations of their scope of competence and seek out training related to parents, married clients, and the role of sports in mental health

    c. **CORRECT.** No action is called for; proceed with assessment and treatment

    d. **Incorrect.** Review and discuss the clinical implications of all known differences

While it may make sense to discuss the clinical implications of these differences (D), remember that this exam is focused on the LMFT's legal and ethical responsibilities. In this instance, the symptoms presented point to a likely diagnosis of major depressive disorder, which should be well within the scope of competence of any licensed therapist ©. Differences in personality, hobbies, or even demographics *in and of themselves* do not necessarily indicate a scope of competence problem; there is nothing in the question to indicate that the therapist would have difficulty treating the client based on any of these factors. So there's no obligation to seek additional training in them (B) or to refer the client out (A).

28. After several months of therapy, a client and their MFT decide together that treatment has been successful and it is time to move toward termination. They have a couple of sessions focused on carrying the client's gains forward. At what was supposed to be the final session, the client expresses hesitation, and says that they would rather keep coming to therapy indefinitely. How can the MFT best manage their ethical responsibility in this case?

    a.   **Incorrect.** Agree to a limited number of additional sessions, and amend the treatment plan

    b.   **Incorrect.** Gradually increase the client's fee as a behavioral nudge toward termination

    c.   **Incorrect.** Agree to continue therapy indefinitely, as long as the client wants it

    d.   **CORRECT.** Assess whether there is any potential benefit to additional sessions, and if not, proceed with termination

Termination is not only appropriate, but ethically required when the therapist does not believe the client has anything to gain by continuing to attend. The therapist should assess whether this is the case, and if there are no further gains to be had, move forward with termination (D). The simple fact that a client wants therapy does not necessarily mean they need or will benefit from it, and seeing a client without even the expectation of benefit © is ethically prohibited. (A) here is simply a shorter-term version of (C) and suffers the same concerns. (B) would likely be considered an exploitation of the client's anxiety around leaving therapy.

29. An MFT is struggling with what they perceive to be unfair treatment by agency administrators. They have had multiple meetings with the MFT to document her steadily declining clinical outcomes and productivity, and concerns about "erratic behavior" raised by coworkers. The MFT acknowledges that they have always been eccentric, but says that clients seem to appreciate and relate to this. The MFT is unaware of other clinicians at the agency being called in for similar meetings. In a recent session, the MFT said to a client, "I don't know why you keep coming here. The people who run this place are awful." How should the MFT proceed?

   a. **CORRECT.** Seek out treatment for the issues interfering with her work
   b. **Incorrect.** Seek out an attorney to address potential labor law violations by the employer
   c. **Incorrect.** Provide clients with information about other community agencies where they can seek help
   d. **Incorrect.** Document the meetings with administrators and share her concerns with her clinical supervisor

While discussing such matters with a supervisor (D) is always a good idea, considering the seriousness of the concerns raised here and the multiple attempts the agency has made to address them, simply discussing them with a supervisor is likely not adequate. Our ethics codes demand that we recognize impairment in ourselves, and take appropriate action when such impairment becomes evident (A), as it clearly has here. Steering clients away from treatment at the agency (C) would be an act of retaliation against the agency, one that is likely not in clients' best interests. And there is nothing in the question to suggest violations of labor law (B); it sounds instead like the agency is doing all they can to address concerns directly and properly.

30. An MFT is working with a client in a different part of the state, one the MFT has never visited, via telemedicine. During a session taking place via videoconference, the client informs the therapist that he recently lost his job and is struggling to navigate the complex web of social services in his area. He fears losing his home in a matter of weeks. Ethically, the MFT should:

    a. **Incorrect.** Volunteer to serve as the client's case manager to better coordinate his services. *Taking on a case manager role might be appropriate if the MFT knows resources local to the client, but that is not the case here.*

    b. **Incorrect.** Travel to where the client is located to provide services in person on a temporary basis. *This would be unreasonable to ask of the therapist, who is certainly not obligated to do so.*

    c. **CORRECT.** Reconsider whether telemedicine services are appropriate for this client. *This best summarizes the MFT's specific ethical responsibility in this case. We are required to evaluate whether telemedicine services are appropriate to the client's needs. In this case, the client's needs have changed, and so a reassessment of that question is appropriate.*

    d. **Incorrect.** Assess for suicidality and substance use. *Assessing for suicidality may be appropriate given the job loss and potential loss of the home, but this is a clinical consideration and not an ethical one. The question is asking specifically for ethical considerations. Nothing in the question suggests substance use.*

31. A client family has been struggling with financial needs since the father was furloughed from her job at a car wash. The family is in therapy to address areas of acculturation and family conflict. There are four boys in the family, ranging in ages from 3 to 13. While all of the family members sometimes come to therapy in dirty, torn clothes, the 8-year-old boy seems particularly withdrawn. He appears underweight, and says that the family sometimes waits for him to go to sleep before they eat dinner. "That's not right," the mother protests. "We send you to bed without dinner when you disobey." The mother expresses her frustration that the 8-year-old is frequently sick and needs to stay home from school. To resolve the MFT's legal obligations, the MFT should:

    a. **Incorrect.** Understand the impact of poverty and possible acculturation trauma
    b. **Incorrect.** Assess the family for violence
    c. **CORRECT.** Report suspected child neglect
    d. **Incorrect.** Ask the mother to provide a release allowing the MFT to review the 8-year-old's medical file

It's important to understand the difference between a task that is clinically appropriate and one that is a legal or ethical obligation. Here, assessing for violence (B) and reviewing medical records (D) both may be appropriate, but neither is required. Understanding the impact of poverty and acculturation (A) is an ethical responsibility, not a legal one. The child is showing clear evidence of neglect, and reporting that suspected neglect (C) is the only option here that reflects a legal obligation.

32. After several sessions of individual therapy focused on anger management, a client becomes visibly angry at his therapist. "I thought you knew what you were doing," the client says. "You misled me." The client pulls a brochure from his pocket and slams it on the table. It's a brochure the MFT is using to advertise his practice, and it describes the MFT as providing psychotherapy focused on anger and resentment issues. It also includes recommendations from two colleagues. Legally, the MFT should:

    a. **CORRECT.** Consider whether the client might have reasonably believed the MFT has more training or experience in anger management than he does

    b. **Incorrect.** Revise the brochure to remove the testimonials

    c. **Incorrect.** Revise the brochure to remove the word "psychotherapy"

    d. **Incorrect.** Consider termination

The recommendations from colleagues are not the same as testimonials from clients and do not need to be removed (B). It's perfectly legal for MFTs to call themselves psychotherapists and describe their work as psychotherapy (C). And termination here (D) would be premature; this may very well be a rift in the relationship that can be healed. MFTs have a legal responsibility to not put out any advertising that is false or misleading. In this case, since the client is reporting that they feel they were misled, the MFT should consider whether that's a reasonable response to the advertising material (A), and if it is, change the material accordingly.

33. An Hispanic family approaches an MFT for family-based treatment. The MFT soon learns that several family members have their own individual therapists, and the parents in the family have a couple therapist who is working with them on their relationship. The family insists that these efforts are all in support of one another, and the family therapy would be to address family conflict and rule-setting. The family offers to pay the MFT the full fee, and insists they would attend every scheduled session. The MFT should:

a. **Incorrect.** Inform the family that family therapy cannot take place until after the individual and couple therapy processes have concluded

b. **Incorrect.** Inform the family that family therapy would be best conducted by the couple therapist, as that therapist is already familiar with the parents and can support them effectively in their parenting

c. **Incorrect.** Require that the family sign releases allowing for contact with the other therapists, and proceed with family therapy only if all other therapists involved agree

d. **CORRECT.** Ask the family to sign releases allowing for consultation and coordination with the other therapists, and proceed with family therapy

Under current ethical guidelines, it is permissible for this MFT to engage in family therapy with this family even while concurrent psychotherapy is taking place with other therapists, ruling out (A) and (B). The MFT does not need to get the other therapists' permission to engage in family therapy (C). Coordinating the services being provided (D) is not a requirement, but is ethically encouraged, and ensures that none of the therapies are promoting contradictory goals.

34. An MFT returns to work several weeks after a severe knee injury. She finds it difficult to focus during sessions because of the amount of pain she is experiencing, and does not remember much of each session after it has concluded. She finds her pain level increasing during the day. The MFT should:

    a. **Incorrect.** Assume this is part of the recovery process, and function as best as she can until the pain subsides. *The MFT's difficulty with focus and memory are impacting her ability to practice. She should be aware of her limitations and ensure that clients are receiving adequate professional care.*

    b. **Incorrect.** Consult with other MFTs who have dealt with physical injuries. *This consultation may be helpful but does not address the fact that her clients are receiving substandard care.*

    c. **CORRECT.** Discontinue seeing clients until the pain is more manageable, making appropriate arrangements for continuity of care. *Of the options available, only this response addresses the impact her injury is having on client care.*

    d. **Incorrect.** Consult with her physician, and ask clients to sign a waiver stating that they understand she is dealing with an injury. *Clients cannot simply sign away their right, and the MFT's responsibility, to competent professional care.*

35. In group supervision, several MFT associates and their supervisor (who is a licensed MFT) are discussing whether the client of one of the associates should make a report of suspected child abuse. The associate who has seen the client says she does not believe the situation warrants a report. The other associates believe there is enough information to form reasonable suspicion of abuse, based on what the associate who has seen the client has said in describing the case. The supervisor validates the arguments being made by both sides, and after a long discussion, their positions are unchanged. The Associate MFT who has seen the case should:

a. **CORRECT.** Make a report of suspected child abuse. *The legal definition of "reasonable suspicion" says, essentially, that if other similar professionals presented with the same information would reasonably suspect abuse, then so should you. In this case, several other similar professionals suspect abuse based on the information available. (The supervisor has not taken a stance on either side.) In fact, everyone in the room who has expressed an opinion believes the case should be reported except the treating MFT. A report should be made.*

b. **Incorrect.** Defer a decision on reporting until she can conduct further assessment. *Once reasonable suspicion has been determined, the decision to report is made and should not be deferred.*

c. **Incorrect.** Hold to her belief that a report is not warranted unless new information comes to light that would change her view. *Based on the opinions of others in the room, she needs to change her view and make a report.*

d. **Incorrect.** Consult with the local child protective service agency. *Such a consultation may be helpful but is not definitive. Based on the MFT's experience in supervision, reasonable suspicion of abuse exists and a report must be made.*

36. An individual client tells an MFT that she is in fear of her husband. The couple has a long history of severe intimate partner violence, and there are protective orders in place requiring that they couple stay away from each other except when meeting in supervised locations to hand off their children. Now that the couple is finally divorcing, the husband has begun leaving threatening voicemails. The client plays one such voicemail for the MFT, who agrees that the client may be in danger. The MFT should:

    a.   **Incorrect.** Notify law enforcement and warn the victim. *The victim is aware of the danger. The MFT does not need to notify law enforcement as the dangerous person is not a client.*

    b.   **Incorrect.** Attempt to contact the husband to reduce the danger. *Without a release, this could be a violation of confidentiality; in any event, reducing the danger in this case is not a responsibility of the MFT.*

    c.   **CORRECT.** Encourage the client to notify law enforcement. *The client has the information needed to notify law enforcement.*

    d.   **Incorrect.** Notify the court that the husband is violating the protective order. *MFTs are neither obligated nor authorized to make such a report in this instance. The client may notify the court if she chooses.*

37. An MFT has received written permission from a former client family to use video of their sessions in group supervision. The MFT is interested in using segments from the videos as part of a workshop at an upcoming therapy conference. The MFT wonders whether the previous permission would apply to the conference setting, but is unable to reach the family, as the family has moved out of state. Ethically, the MFT should:

   a. **CORRECT.** Only use the video segments at the conference if the MFT obtains specific written permission from the clients. *Such uses require client permission in writing. If the MFT is going to use existing recordings in a new way not previously authorized, then a new written permission is needed.*

   b. **Incorrect.** Only use the video segments at the conference if the MFT edits the videos such that none of the clients use any client names during the segments shown. *Particularly on video, observers may determine client identity even when names are not being used. This action is not sufficient to ensure confidentiality.*

   c. **Incorrect.** Only use the video segments at the conference if the MFT obtains written declarations from each workshop attendee that they will keep the contents of the workshop confidential. *It is up to the clients to provide or withhold permission for the video's use, not up to the audience to allow it.*

   d. **Incorrect.** Only use the video segments at the conference if the number of attendees at the workshop is comparable to the typical number of attendees in group supervision. *The fact that a comparable number of people are involved does not mean that the usage of the recordings is the same. A new written authorization is needed.*

38. An MFT is brought in as an expert witness in a criminal case where a woman was accused of violently beating her 8-year-old daughter. The MFT is asked by the court to speak on the long-term effects of child abuse, as well as on factors that can lead mothers to become abusive. The MFT has expertise in these areas. The MFT also finds the behavior that the woman is accused of repugnant. The MFT should:

a. **Incorrect.** Speak solely about what the MFT knows about the specific case being tried, and avoid speaking in generalities. *Expert witnesses should not speak on the specific case being tried. They are used to provide the court with expert knowledge on relevant subject matter.*

b. **CORRECT.** Speak solely from her knowledge and expertise in the field, and avoid saying anything about the specific case being tried. *This is the appropriate role of an expert witness in a court proceeding.*

c. **Incorrect.** Clarify for the court that no explanatory factors for abuse should be understood as making child abuse acceptable. *This is a moral, and not a scientific, stance. MFTs in court proceedings are required to speak from their knowledge and expertise.*

d. **Incorrect.** Investigate the merits of the case before determining how to testify. *Expert witnesses are not called on to testify about the merits of a particular case.*

39. An MFT is doing an intake session with an individual client who begins discussing her family life. The MFT realizes that the client's spouse is someone the MFT had dated 10 years ago. The MFT remembers that relationship fondly, and is pleased to learn that the person the MFT had dated went on to get married. Ethically, the MFT should:

a. **Incorrect.** Immediately disclose the MFT's realization and discuss with the client how they should proceed. *Resolution of an ethical concern may involve client input, but in this instance the obligation on the MFT is clear and resolution of the issue does not require or accept client input.*

b. **CORRECT.** Inform the client that the MFT cannot work with this client, and provide appropriate referrals. *The CAMFT Code of Ethics specifically prohibits MFTs from entering into a therapeutic relationship with the partner or family member of someone with whom the MFT had a prior sexual relationship. Because this is an intake session, there is not a significant therapeutic relationship to seek to preserve. Termination and referrals are appropriate.*

c. **Incorrect.** Evaluate whether the length of time since the relationship and the current fondness toward the client's spouse are sufficient to ensure that the therapy with this client would not be impacted. *These considerations are not relevant. The MFT is ethically prohibited from working with this client.*

d. **Incorrect.** No action is called for. *Specific action in the form of termination is called for here.*

40. The client of an MFT has been engaged in a difficult custody battle over her two sons. The client has shown the MFT photos, emails and text messages her husband has sent her, where he regularly talks about being drunk and often appears intoxicated. Though the children are all healthy, the client expresses fear for her children's safety around the father, and asks the MFT to inform the court that her husband may have a substance use disorder. The MFT should:

    a. **Incorrect.** Consider whether a report of child neglect is appropriate. *While the husband's behavior is potentially troubling, simple use of a substance in and of itself – without evidence that the use has occurred in the presence of the children, and without evidence that they have been harmed or endangered – would not be enough to support a report of suspected neglect.*

    b. **Incorrect.** Refuse to review these photos, emails, and text messages in the future, focusing instead on the client's reaction to them. *The information may be clinically relevant. There is no obligation to discontinue reviewing them.*

    c. **Incorrect.** Provide the court with a letter stating that, based on the limited information available, the MFT believes the husband may have a substance use disorder and should be further assessed. *Given the likely impact of such a letter in the custody proceeding, the MFT should be extremely cautious about offering a diagnosis of someone the MFT has not personally assessed or treated.*

    d. **CORRECT.** Refuse the client's request. *Given the likely impact of such a letter in the custody proceeding, the MFT should be extremely cautious about offering a diagnosis of someone the MFT has not personally assessed or treated. The simple fact that someone regularly uses a substance is not sufficient for a diagnosis of Substance Use Disorder.*

41. The client of an MFT comes to therapy with a wide smile, eager to tell the MFT what happened over the weekend. The client, who is 57, took her mother, who suffers from dementia, to see the Grand Canyon for the first time as a surprise birthday gift. The client reports that the mother angrily protested at first, not understanding why she was leaving her room at her nursing home. Once in the car, the client reports that her mother did not understand where they were going. But when her mother saw the Grand Canyon, the client reported "she was speechless. She was in awe." The MFT should:

    a. **CORRECT.** Report suspected elder abuse to the local adult protective services agency
    b. **Incorrect.** Direct the conversation back to issues relevant to the client's treatment
    c. **Incorrect.** Assess for potential elder abuse
    d. **Incorrect.** Ask the client to sign a Release of Information allowing the MFT to contact the mother and check on her current condition

Taking an elder or dependent adult out of the state against their will is the definition of abduction as a form of elder or dependent adult abuse (A). This must be reported. At this point in the session, the therapist has enough information to reasonably suspect abuse, so redirecting to clinical issues (B) does not resolve the MFT's legal mandate. There is no need to assess further for abuse (C), it can be reported based on the information available. And while the mother may be able to speak to the impact of this event on her (D) – and to whatever degree she can, she may say the impact was positive – it is not her response but the action itself that determines whether elder abuse has occurred.

42. A client has seen his MFT twice in the therapist's office. Before the third session, the client calls the MFT as the client is running late. The client asks whether the start of the session can be conducted via phone, with the understanding that he will arrive at the office about 20 minutes after the scheduled starting time. The MFT should:

    a.   **Incorrect.** Inform the client that the session can begin when he arrives at the office

    b.   **CORRECT.** Inform the clients of the risks and benefits of engaging in telehealth, and seek the client's consent for this form of treatment

    c.   **Incorrect.** Conduct the initial 20 minutes of the session by phone

    d.   **Incorrect.** Inform the client that while a phone session is prohibited, it would be possible to meet via real-time, two-way videoconferencing, either for the first 20 minutes or for the full session

By state law, clients must specifically consent to the use of telehealth services, after having been informed of the risks (B). It would not be legal to conduct any therapy via telehealth (C) before securing this consent. A phone call is a legally allowed technology for therapy, eliminating both (A) and (D) as response options.

43. An MFT who identifies as gay is working in an agency setting, and conducting an initial assessment session with a client who also identifies as gay. The client tells the MFT that he feels very trusting toward the MFT because they are both part of the LGBTQ community, so "I know you understand what I've gone through." The client becomes tearful at several points in the assessment, and on other occasions, the MFT believes the client is actively flirting with him. The MFT should:

a. **Incorrect.** Provide the client a copy of the brochure *Therapy Never Includes Sexual Behavior*

b. **Incorrect.** Transfer the client to a different therapist within the agency

c. **CORRECT.** Understand the client behavior as part of the clinical picture and inquire about trauma history

d. **Incorrect.** Consult with a colleague to minimize countertransference and ensure the MFT can maintain proper boundaries

Consulting (D) is an appropriate protective measure to take when there is evidence of the need for such a measure. In this instance, there is no evidence that the MFT is experiencing countertransference, or that the MFT is having (or is likely to have) difficulty maintaining proper boundaries. Transferring the client (B) is similarly unsupported. The MFT is ethically obligated to maintain awareness of marginalized groups, including the LGBTQIA+ community, and the impacts of oppression and discrimination (C). In this instance, the MFT's primary obligation is to better understand the client's behavior within the client's broader social context. There is no evidence here that the client had any sexual relationship with a prior therapist, so there is no need to provide the brochure (A).

44. An MFT takes notes during sessions in order to track key moments in session and important words or phrases used by various clients. The MFT keeps these handwritten notes separate from clients' files. The MFT receives a court order for all available treatment records on one of the MFT's clients. That client has an extensive file, as the MFT had seen the client for more than 100 sessions. The MFT should:

    a.   **Incorrect.** Respond to the court order by asserting privilege. *A court order must be obeyed. The MFT could assert privilege in response to a subpoena, but the fact that it is a court order suggests that a judge has already determined that the records must be provided.*

    b.   **Incorrect.** Respond to the court order by providing a treatment summary. *The court order was for "all available treatment records," so a summary would be an insufficient response.*

    c.   **Incorrect.** Respond to the court order by providing the full file for the client, without the handwritten notes that had been kept separately. *While the handwritten notes may fall under the definition of "psychotherapy notes" in HIPAA that is different from the client's medical record, both types of records are subject to subpoena or court order. When a court order demands all available treatment records, both types of records must be provided.*

    d.   **CORRECT.** Respond to the court order by providing the full file for the client and all handwritten notes pertaining to the client's sessions. *This is a full and appropriate response in keeping with the court order.*

45. An MFT is working with a religious family whose son has been diagnosed with a blood disorder. While not fatal, the disorder could significantly impact the boy's growth and development. The family tells you that after meeting with multiple doctors, they have elected to use only spiritual healing for their son, and to put his health "in God's hands." The MFT should:

   a. **Incorrect.** Advise the clients to utilize Western medicine techniques known to treat the disorder. *This would be providing medical advice, which is outside the MFT scope of practice.*

   b. **Incorrect.** Report suspected child abuse. *There is no evidence of abuse in the question. See option C below for consideration of neglect.*

   c. **Incorrect.** Report suspected child neglect. *State law provides an exception to the definition of neglect. That exception allows parents to choose spiritual or religious-based treatment for their children as long as they have met with a physician who has assessed the child and the parents' decisions are "informed and appropriate."*

   d. **CORRECT.** Discuss with the family how they reached their decision and what its possible impacts could be. *State law provides an exception to the definition of neglect. That exception allows parents to choose spiritual or religious-based treatment for their children as long as they have met with a physician who has assessed the child and the parents' decisions are "informed and appropriate."*

46. An MFT has been working with a family to improve the parents' skills in managing their daughters' behavior. The family experiences frequent crises, and the MFT considers it her most difficult case. On the day before the MFT is scheduled to leave for a two-week vacation out of state, one of the daughters in the family admits to frequent drug use and self-injury. The parents call the MFT in a panic and ask for an emergency session. The MFT assesses the family by phone and determines that no one in the family is immediately suicidal or homicidal, though the parents are concerned that the daughter may become suicidal. The MFT should:

a. **Incorrect.** Cancel or delay the planned vacation and attend to the urgent needs of the family. *This would be a demonstration of weak boundaries. The family may learn that crises are the way to become more important to the therapist.*

b. **Incorrect.** Plan on conducting at least occasional phone check-ins while she is on vacation to ensure family stability. *This level of response is insufficient to the family's immediate needs.*

c. **CORRECT.** Work with the family to arrange for a colleague to fill in for the MFT while on vacation, assessing the family and carrying the treatment plan forward. *This best balances therapeutic boundaries with the family's need for additional assessment and intervention.*

d. **Incorrect.** Report suspected child neglect based on the daughter's drug use and self-injury, which the family has not adequately protected her from. *The family sought treatment as soon as they became aware of these issues, suggesting that they are managing the situation appropriately.*

47. An MFT has been seeing an individual client for three months. The client is struggling with post-traumatic stress following a military deployment. While the client is in therapy, the MFT gets to know the client's spouse, as the client signs a Release of Information allowing the MFT and the spouse to share information about the client's symptoms, treatment, and billing. Three months into the therapy, the MFT and the client's spouse encounter each other at a bar. They have sex that night. Legally, the MFT must now:

    a. **Incorrect.** Terminate the sexual relationship immediately, terminate the client relationship immediately, and self-report to the BBS

    b. **Incorrect.** Terminate the sexual relationship immediately, and immediately disclose the encounter to the client

    c. **Incorrect.** Terminate the sexual relationship immediately, encourage the client's spouse to disclose the encounter to the client, and provide the client a copy of the brochure *Therapy Never Includes Sexual Behavior*

    d. **CORRECT.** Take steps to minimize the emotional harm that may come to the client as a result of the encounter

This is a tougher one than it at first appears to be. While our codes of ethics prohibit sexual relationships with a client's spouse or family member, state law on the topic limits the prohibition to clients themselves. So the MFT doesn't have a specific *legal* obligation to end the sexual relationship. However, within the unprofessional conduct statutes, there is a prohibition against "intentionally or recklessly causing physical or emotional harm to any client." In this case, the sexual encounter almost surely would be considered to violate that law – but the act has already happened, and the question asks what the MFT is legally obligated to do *now*. The MFT needs to carefully consider next steps so as to not do more intentional or reckless harm to this client. The appropriate steps that meet that need may vary by the specific context of the case. Providing the client a copy of the brochure © is not a legal requirement in these circumstances; immediately disclosing the encounter to the client (B) may be inappropriate and cause further harm; and self-report to the BBS (A) is not a legal obligation when an MFT has violated a legal standard. The only response option that accurately captures the MFT's *current, legal* obligations in this scenario is (D).

48. A week after a particularly difficult session, a client arrives on time for her session with an MFT in the early afternoon. She brings a sandwich for the MFT, and offers it at the beginning of the session. She also pulls out a sandwich for herself, and asks whether it is OK for them both to eat during session. The MFT should:

a. **Incorrect.** Politely refuse the offer and consider moving the client's sessions to a different time of day. *Whether the therapist accepts the offer or not, moving sessions to a different time of day would be an indirect way of managing boundary considerations. Better to manage boundaries directly and openly with the client than to arbitrarily exercise power in this way.*

b. **Incorrect.** Accept the sandwich and conduct the session over lunch, supporting the client's autonomy. *This may be appropriate in some settings (see rationale for option D below) but also risks relaxing boundaries in therapy. Therefore it cannot be concluded that this is a generally acceptable option.*

c. **Incorrect.** Refuse the gift, but allow the client to have lunch in session to provide her with a sense of comfort and safety. *This sends a mixed message to the client about what behavior is appropriate in session – refusing a small gift suggests strict boundaries, while allowing the client to eat in session suggests loose boundaries – and would be awkward at best for both parties.*

d. **CORRECT.** Consider and discuss the larger ramifications for therapy. *While there would be boundary questions to consider here, context matters a great deal. In some recovery-oriented settings, a session over lunch might be normal and accepted. In other contexts, it might represent a dangerous shift in boundaries toward a more informal, friendly relationship with the client. Concerns should be directly discussed.*

49. A client asks to use her insurance to pay for therapy with an MFT, as she would not be able to pay out of pocket. The client's husband works for a large multinational corporation, and the client's insurance is provided through that corporation. The client tells the MFT that she believes she may have Borderline Personality Disorder and Substance Use Disorder, and does not want her husband or the corporation to learn of these diagnoses. The MFT should:

a.   **Incorrect.** Provide referrals to low-fee clinics. *It is possible that the client does not qualify for the diagnoses she fears, and that she could receive insurance coverage for treatment without her diagnoses being revealed. Referrals at this point would be premature.*

b.   **CORRECT.** Discuss what information is provided to insurers, and what the client's treatment options may be. *MFTs are ethically obligated to review what information is shared with third-party payors. Reviewing the client's treatment options in that context is appropriate.*

c.   **Incorrect.** Contact the insurer to advocate for the client. *While professional ethics support advocating for clients with third-party payors, first it must be determined what needs advocating. If the client does not qualify for the diagnoses she fears, if diagnoses are not necessary for the insurer to pay for treatment, or if the insurer would not share the diagnoses as a matter of current policy, no advocacy would be necessary.*

d.   **Incorrect.** Advise the client to seek a court order that will seal her treatment records. *This would be giving legal advice, which is outside of the MFT's scope of practice.*

50. An MFT encounters a former client from many years ago at a party. They enjoy catching up socially, and are each impressed with the other. In the time since therapy, the former client has been married and divorced. The MFT, also now divorced, finds herself seeing the former client as an equal. She also finds herself attracted to the former client. Ethically, the MFT should:

    a. **Incorrect.** Provide the former client with a copy of the brochure *Therapy Never Includes Sexual Behavior. This is a legal requirement when a client informs a therapist that the client had a sexual relationship with a prior therapist.*

    b. **Incorrect.** Assess whether the former client also sees the MFT as an equal, and if so, consider initiating a romantic relationship. *The AAMFT Code of Ethics now makes the prohibition against sexual relationships with former clients a lifetime prohibition. The CAMFT Code of Ethics, while keeping the absolute prohibition at two years, goes on to acknowledge that such relationships remain problematic even after that timeframe.*

    c. **Incorrect.** Review the reasons why the client sought therapy years ago, and determine whether the former client has truly resolved those concerns. *This is not relevant to consideration of whether to initiate a romantic relationship.*

    d. **CORRECT.** Limit her social contact with the former client. *Of the options available, only this option recognizes the potential for harm in a sexual relationship with a former client and acts in response to that potential.*

51. An MFT has been working with a family for several sessions and plans a session where the entire family will participate in a ceremony relieving the oldest daughter of the responsibility she has taken on as a co-parent. Shortly before the session, the mother informs the MFT that she will be away on a business trip and asks whether she can participate in the session by phone or videoconferencing. The mother's frequent absences are part of the reason why the daughter felt obligated to take on parenting tasks. The MFT should:

   a. **Incorrect.** Contact the BBS to see whether the MFT can include the mother in session while she is on her trip. *The BBS does not provide legal advice, and even asking the question may require providing information that is confidential.*
   b. **Incorrect.** Include the mother in the session and in the ceremony via phone or videoconference, and clarify that her involvement is consultation rather than therapy. *Simply calling the mother's involvement consultation does not make it something different from therapy. This is especially true considering that the entire purpose of her presence in session is to be involved in a therapeutic intervention that the MFT designed.*
   c. **CORRECT.** Refuse the mother's request and reschedule the ceremony for a time she can attend in person. *MFTs are required to carefully assess whether telemedicine services are appropriate in a given case. Here, the mother's absence would likely have a major impact on the planned ceremony; having her participate by phone or videoconference rather than in person appears likely to impact the effectiveness of the intervention.*
   d. **Incorrect.** Contact the other family members to see whether they believe including the mother would be appropriate. *While the family may be able to offer useful clinical feedback on this question, it is not the role of the family to resolve the MFT's legal and ethical concerns.*

52. In an effort to address systemic racism and oppression in US society, an MFT decides to create three slots in her weekly schedule that she will use to provide no-fee therapy to African-American clients. She announces this with a flyer in her office. A Latino client asks whether he would also be eligible for one of those slots. The MFT should:

    a.   **Incorrect.** Ask the Latino client to demonstrate how the oppression he has experienced is comparable to that of African-Americans

    b.   **Incorrect.** Immediately agree to make the slot available to the Latino client as well, clarifying that it is open to all those who identify as people of color

    c.   **CORRECT.** Expand eligibility for these slots to include anyone who has experienced systemic oppression

    d.   **Incorrect.** Clarify that because of African-Americans' unique position in US society, these slots are only open to those who classify themselves as African-American

While there is no doubt that the MFT is well-intentioned here – and there is a great argument to be made that such a program *should* be allowed – it is unethical and illegal to create racial preferences in pricing the MFT's services. Limiting free slots just to those who classify as African-American (D) or who identify as people of color (B), or providing African-Americans with automatic eligibility while requiring others to prove their worthiness (A), would violate legal and ethical standards that prohibit discrimination on the basis of race. The only workable option here is to focus program eligibility on personal experience (C), which is not a protected class in non-discrimination standards.

53. An MFT and their client disagree about how the client should handle an upcoming family reunion. The client has a history of problematic alcohol use leading to hospitalization. The MFT is concerned that the large amounts of alcohol likely to be served at the reunion could be triggering for the client, perhaps even leading to a relapse. The client is confident in their sobriety, and interested in seeing family members for the purposes of addressing past conflict. The MFT should:

   a. **CORRECT.** Argue strongly in support of the client not attending the reunion, while empathizing with the client's desire to attend and clarifying that it is the client's choice to make
   b. **Incorrect.** Considering the level of risk involved, make it a condition of continuing treatment that the client not attend the reunion
   c. **Incorrect.** Inquire about the client's reasons for wanting to attend the reunion in the presence of these risks
   d. **Incorrect.** Understand that the decision of whether to attend is the client's alone to make, and therefore do not raise the MFT's concerns in session

The ethical prohibition against making major life decisions for clients is sometimes misunderstood as a complete ban on advice-giving. But MFTs can and should provide clients with advice based on the MFT's professional opinion, when it is appropriate to do so. This is an instance where it is appropriate to do so, considering the client's history and apparent disregard for what the MFT understandably views as risks. The MFT should of course not make this about the client taking care of the therapist, but empathizing with the client's wishes and clarifying that it is the client's decision to make (A) should strike that balance well. Making it a condition of treatment that the client not attend the reunion (B) is not ethically appropriate here, as it misuses the therapist's position in an attempt to force the client to agree with the MFT's preferred decision. Options (C) and (D) here do not include the therapist assisting with the client decision-making process, and thus are inadequate to the situation at hand.

54. An MFT becomes seriously ill and is hospitalized, with the expectation that the hospitalization will be long-term. The MFT is suffering serious pain and difficulty with cognition due to the combination of medications the MFT is being given. The MFT has an active caseload of about 20 clients, some of whom are at risk for going into crisis and require regular contact. Under the circumstances, the MFT should:

    a. **Incorrect.** Conduct telehealth sessions from the MFT's hospital room until clients can be transferred

    b. **Incorrect.** Sell the MFT's practice, including its current active caseload, and inform clients in writing that as of the sale date, they will be attending sessions with the new practice owner

    c. **CORRECT.** Authorize another qualified clinician to access client records and coordinate continuity of care

    d. **Incorrect.** Send a letter to each client releasing them from the MFT's care and closing their cases

This is a difficult situation because there is no good solution. The MFT's symptoms suggest that the MFT will not be able to provide minimally competent care, so they should not be conducting sessions (A). And since no one "owns" a client – clients have autonomy to choose their own providers – the MFT is not in a position to dictate to clients who they will be attending future sessions with (B). To avoid client abandonment, the MFT must do more than just sending clients a letter closing their cases (D). Option (C) addresses continuity of care needs by essentially doing a professional will, authorizing another therapist to take over while the MFT is incapacitated. While you may initially be concerned about confidentiality in this approach, remember that clinicians who are actively involved on a client's treatment team can share records for the purposes of treatment planning, even without a client release.

55. An MFT is treating an adolescent client who was mandated to therapy by the juvenile court system following a series of convictions for shoplifting, truancy, and other low-level offenses. The MFT has been treating the adolescent for six sessions with moderate progress when the client provides the MFT with a form from the court that the MFT is supposed to complete in order to evaluate the client's participation and progress in therapy. The form specifically asks the MFT to evaluate the client's preparedness to be released from probation. The form says it is to be returned by the MFT to the juvenile probation office. The MFT should:

    a. **Incorrect.** Decline to complete the form
    b. **CORRECT.** Complete those sections of the form that relate to dates of service and topics of therapy, while leaving evaluative questions blank
    c. **Incorrect.** Complete the form and return it to the client to submit to the juvenile probation office
    d. **Incorrect.** Complete the form and return it to the juvenile probation office as instructed

The MFT is right to be careful about the distinction between a treating therapist and an evaluator. Our ethics codes demand that we keep those roles separate. However, communication with the probation office is allowed, so long as the MFT remains in the treating-therapist role. The MFT could safely complete information about dates of service and topics of therapy without serving as an evaluator for probation purposes.

56. A client comes to an MFT and identifies herself as the victim of intimate partner violence. She describes instances of her husband physically assaulting her and threatening her with a gun. She tells the MFT that her husband is a police officer who is skilled with technology and monitors their bank accounts closely. She asks the MFT to see her on a cash-only basis with no physical receipts, and to not keep any records of her treatment, as she is worried those records could be used by her husband to discover where she is currently staying and to describe her in future divorce proceedings as mentally unfit for custody of their children. Considering the MFT's ethical responsibilities, the MFT should:

    a.   **Incorrect.** Agree to the client's requests

    b.   **Incorrect.** Agree to the client's requests surrounding payment, and inform her that clinical records must be kept, but that those records will not include any information about her mental health

    c.   **Incorrect.** Agree to the client's requests surrounding payment, and inform the client that records from treatment of intimate partner violence are not subject to subpoena

    d.   **CORRECT.** Inform the client that neither of her requests can be honored

There are a lot of pieces we could unpack here, as there are potentially workable options outside of what is presented in the response choices. However, of the choices here, the best one is (D). We rule out (A) because clinical record-keeping is an ethical requirement; the clinician cannot agree to an arrangement where no records will be created. We rule out (B) and (C) because both contain incorrect elements. If the client has active mental health concerns, it would not be adequate to document her treatment without documenting those concerns (B). And California law offers no exception to subpoena for records relating to intimate partner violence (C). You could make an argument for alternate arrangements here that involve clinical-recordkeeping without financial recordkeeping (recall that the CAMFT and AAMFT codes disagree in whether financial records are specifically necessary), but considering the options available here, (D) is the only one that works.

57. A young adult seeks the services of an MFT to help him determine his life path. He specifically asks the MFT to help him learn how to perform household tasks like laundry and help with financial management, explaining that since he had spent many years in a series of foster homes as a child, he never learned these skills. The MFT should:

    a.   **CORRECT.** Turn away the client and refer him to community resources. *The client is seeking services outside of the MFT's scope of practice.*

    b.   **Incorrect.** Turn away the client and refer him to three other therapists. *The client is presenting with goals that are not appropriate for psychotherapy.*

    c.   **Incorrect.** Accept the client and focus on the skills he is asking to learn. *The client is presenting with goals that are not appropriate for psychotherapy.*

    d.   **Incorrect.** Accept the client and focus on the trauma he suffered in the foster care system. *The simple fact that the client was involved in the foster care system does not necessarily mean that he was traumatized by that involvement.*

58. An Associate MFT is working for an LMFT in private practice. The Associate is interested in practicing via telehealth at some point in the future, and has a number of questions about applicable laws and regulations. The supervisor is not familiar with the current legal rules surrounding telehealth care. Ethically, the supervisor should:

   a. **Incorrect.** Direct the supervisee to research their specific questions, and report back to the supervisor on what they find
   b. **Incorrect.** Discontinue the supervision relationship and refer the associate to a supervisor who practices via telehealth
   c. **CORRECT.** Seek out a training course on current state laws and regulations for telehealth care, and inform the associate of what they learned in the course
   d. **Incorrect.** Inform the supervisee in writing that it is the supervisee's sole responsibility to ensure legal compliance with telehealth rules

Supervisors are ethically obligated to maintain awareness of changes in laws, and to inform supervisees of those changes ©. Directing the supervisee to do this research (A) is placing the supervisor's responsibility on the supervisee. Informing the supervisee in writing that it is the supervisee's job to be legally compliant (D) does not remove the supervisor's responsibility to maintain knowledge of current laws. Even though the supervisor may not be practicing telehealth themselves, and thus there may be a question of competence here, the supervisee simply wants to engage in telehealth "at some point in the future," so immediately ending the supervision relationship (B) is not necessary or appropriate here.

59. A client who has expressed great concern about anyone knowing she is in therapy passes out in the middle of a session. The MFT the client was seeing is able to wake her long enough to learn that she has recently been struggling with illness and has pain from a neck injury, and the MFT knows from the client's intake paperwork that she has a blood disorder. The MFT should:

   a. **Incorrect.** Stay with the client and continue attempting to wake her. *Passing out mid-session may be indicative of a medical emergency. Absent other information, it should be treated as an emergency.*

   b. **Incorrect.** Call 911 and transport the client outside of the office into a public area to protect her privacy. *Calling 911 is appropriate, but attempting to transport the client is not, particularly given her known neck injury.*

   c. **Incorrect.** Call 911 and summon paramedics without providing any information about the client or her illness. *Paramedics may need information on the woman's recent illness and blood disorder in order to treat her appropriately. It is acceptable to share this information with other health care providers in an emergency, and the MFT can do so without revealing anything about the woman's therapy.*

   d. **CORRECT.** Call 911, summon paramedics, and inform them of the client's medical issues. *MFTs are allowed to share medical information in an emergency situation, and the MFT in this instance can do so without revealing any information about the client's therapy.*

60. A couple has been attending therapy for four months with an MFT when they report a recent instance of relationship violence. One partner was left with several scratches and bruises, some of which are visible to the MFT. The other partner, who works as a school administrator, reports also having been injured. The couple largely agrees about what happened, and reports that this event has solidified their commitment to therapy. They have two children, but the children have been staying with their grandparents for the past several days, since before the violent event occurred. In considering the MFT's legal and ethical obligations, the MFT should:

    a. **CORRECT.** Further assess the couple's immediate risk
    b. **Incorrect.** Discontinue couple therapy and proceed with individual sessions
    c. **Incorrect.** Because one partner is a school employee, the violence must be reported to law enforcement
    d. **Incorrect.** Report suspected emotional abuse to a local child protective service agency

Though it is common practice, it is not a legal or ethical requirement to discontinue couple sessions when there has been a recent act of violence (B). In fact, some research suggests that continuing to see the couple together can be done safely and effectively. There is no reporting requirement triggered here, as the children did not witness the event (D) and the employment of the partners does not impact the MFT's reporting responsibilities (C). The MFT should assess immediate risk and take steps necessary to protect the couple's immediate safety (A).

61. A woman who is seeing an MFT for treatment of depression dies under mysterious circumstances. In therapy, she had discussed her recreational drug use, and her fear that her ex-husband may become violent with her. The MFT receives a notice from the local coroner investigating the woman's cause of death that the coroner would like to review the woman's treatment records. The MFT should:

   a. **Incorrect.** Contact the woman's next of kin to determine their wishes
   b. **Incorrect.** Claim privilege on behalf of the client
   c. **Incorrect.** Offer to answer specific questions, but refuse to provide the treatment record
   d. **CORRECT.** Provide the requested records

While most attention for exceptions to confidentiality focuses on the "big four" exceptions, there are other exceptions in state law as well – and a coroner's investigation of the death of a client is one of them. In this case, the MFT is legally obligated to turn over the records (D). It isn't up to the client's next of kin (A). A coroner's investigation is not a judicial proceeding, so privilege does not apply (B). And it doesn't make sense (or comply with the law) for the MFT to serve as a filter of treatment records (C).

62. A middle-aged man who is seeing a psychologist to work on his symptoms of anxiety inquires with an MFT about the possibility of the man and his wife seeing the MFT for couple counseling. The man explains that while some of his anxiety is about how others in his life perceive him, this is improving with treatment and he sees this as being markedly different from the work he and his wife would do with the MFT. The couple have been together for eight years and have two children. The MFT should:

a. **Incorrect.** Defer the request and ask the man to wait for couple counseling until the individual treatment is concluded. *While professional ethics encourage caution and coordination when a client is seeing two therapists simultaneously, it is not prohibited and may be clinically appropriate.*

b. **Incorrect.** Accept the man and his wife as a couple client, and encourage the man to discontinue individual therapy while the couple work is in progress. *While professional ethics encourage caution and coordination when a client is seeing two therapists simultaneously, it is not prohibited and may be clinically appropriate. Discontinuing the individual therapy is not necessary and may be inappropriate.*

c. **CORRECT.** Consider the potential conflicts involved in the man seeing two therapists simultaneously for treatment of issues that may be intertwined. *While professional ethics encourage caution and coordination when a client is seeing two therapists simultaneously, it is not prohibited and may be clinically appropriate.*

d. **Incorrect.** Refuse the request on the grounds that his anxiety is already being appropriately treated. *The anxiety does seem to be receiving appropriate treatment, but the client is asking for assistance with his relationship. Refusing the request for couple therapy on this basis does not make sense.*

63. An MFT learns of a new cross-referral group on a popular social media site. The group is open to all health care professionals. To remain in the group, each person must agree to provide at least one referral a month to at least one other member of the group. A group administrator collects information about these referrals to ensure members are meeting the requirement. That information only includes the member making the referral, the members referred to, and the date, without any client information. The MFT believes joining this group will help build her practice. The MFT should:

a. **Incorrect.** Join the group and make referrals within it, as client confidentiality is protected. *The protection of confidentiality does not change the concern about the MFT receiving payment for referrals (see below) and making referrals based on her own interests rather than those of the client.*

b. **Incorrect.** Join the group and agree to the requirement, but explain to the group administrator that the MFT cannot provide any information on when referrals are made or to whom. *By agreeing to the requirement, the MFT is promising to make referrals that may not be clinically appropriate.*

c. **Incorrect.** Join the group, make her commitment to her professional ethics known, and participate in the group in a manner most adherent to the ethics code possible given the group's requirements. *The group itself is fundamentally not in keeping with the ethics code. While this language can be useful for MFTs figuring out what to do when an **employer's** practice conflicts with the ethics code, here the group is not an employer.*

d. **CORRECT.** Not join the group as it runs counter to her legal responsibilities. *The MFT would be, in effect, receiving payment for referrals, which is a violation of law. The payment would come in the form of continued group membership. Furthermore, this scenario suggests that the MFT would be making referrals based in part on her own interests (in remaining part of the group), rather than making referrals based on what is in the client's best interests. The MFT should not join the group.*

64. A wealthy client who is unfamiliar with therapy approaches an MFT and requests specific accommodations to protect the client's privacy. The client wants the MFT to meet with the client at the client's home for intensive, 3-hour sessions. The client wants the MFT to park on the street, and not in the client's driveway. The client wants the MFT to describe themselves as a florist to any photographers that may be outside the client's home. And the client wants to pay in cash, with no written records of the sessions. Ethically, the MFT should:

    a. **Incorrect.** Refuse to lie to photographers or anyone else about their profession, but agree not to acknowledge that the client is in fact a client

    b. **Incorrect.** Refuse to park on the street, as entering through the client's garage is more appropriate for preserving confidentiality

    c. **CORRECT.** Refuse to agree not to maintain records, while expressing openness about the level of detail to be included in records

    d. **Incorrect.** Refuse to engage in 3-hour sessions because of the possible intensity, and inform the client that therapy sessions cannot run longer than 90 minutes

Our codes of ethics demand "accurate and adequate" records. While the other measures requested by the client may be reasonable, and the MFT could choose whether to agree to them, the request to not have records runs counter to the MFT's ethical responsibilities. It is, however, possible to discuss and find agreement on how much detail is appropriate to include.

65. An MFT with a full practice grows tired of working evenings, but recognizes that only evening times are convenient for many of the families she treats. She may:

   a. **Incorrect.** Take on two associates, and give ongoing clients with evening appointments to the associates. *The MFT could offer to these clients that they transfer to her associates, but cannot mandate such a change. Clients have autonomy in choosing treatment providers and may not be given from one therapist to another.*

   b. **Incorrect.** Express her frustration with evening sessions to her clients, and ask for their assistance in developing solutions. *This is placing the therapist's needs ahead of those of the clients. Relying on clients to resolve the therapist's problem displays poor boundaries.*

   c. **Incorrect.** Discontinue accepting married couples or couples with children in her practice. *This appears to be discrimination based on marital status.*

   d. **CORRECT.** With proper notice, add a $100 surcharge to appointments starting at 6pm or later. *As long as clients understand their fee and the basis on which it is computed, and ongoing clients are given adequate notice of the change, this is acceptable.*

66. An Associate MFT confides in her supervisor, a licensed MFT, that the associate has been having sexual fantasies about the supervisor. She expresses embarrassment about the fantasies and clarifies that she would never act on them, adding that she believes they stem from the supervisor helping her to feel safe as she learns how to be a therapist. The supervisor should:

    a. **Incorrect.** Further explore the reasons behind the fantasies to determine whether they would interfere with the supervisory process. *It is not the supervisor's role to explore the reasons behind the fantasies; doing so confuses supervision for therapy.*

    b. **Incorrect.** Temporarily place the associate with a different supervisor until she is stabilized and able to be more present in supervision. *There is no evidence that the associate is somehow destabilized, or that she is less than present in supervision now.*

    c. **CORRECT.** Praise the associate's courage, direct her to her own therapist, and monitor the associate's behavior in supervision and with clients. *This preserves continuity of care while keeping the roles of supervisor and therapist separate and recognizing that the supervisee brought up an issue that many would find difficult to discuss.*

    d. **Incorrect.** Temporarily remove the associate from client care until further assessment can be completed and the fantasies can be addressed. *There is no evidence in the question that client care has been compromised in any way. Removing her from client care could be considered client abandonment.*

67. A client calls her therapist, an LMFT, from a train headed for Oregon. The LMFT is surprised to learn that the client is calling rather than attending in person, but as it is their scheduled session time, agrees to talk with the client by phone. The client tells the LMFT that she expects the train will cross into Oregon in about 20 minutes, but that there is no way for her to know when exactly that happens. The LMFT should:

    a. **CORRECT.** End the conversation within about 20 minutes. *Assuming that the LMFT is not licensed in Oregon, the LMFT cannot treat the client once the client crosses the state line.*

    b. **Incorrect.** Continue the session for the fully scheduled time. *See option A.*

    c. **Incorrect.** Conduct a crisis assessment and then immediately end the call. *There is no evidence that the client is in crisis; either way, the LMFT could treat the client for as long as the client is in California.*

    d. **Incorrect.** Inquire as to the client's formal state of residency. *The client's state of residency is not relevant when determining whether a California licensed therapist can work with a client who travels out of state.*

68. An LMFT has been working with a client who describes himself as a computer hacker. Sessions have focused on his difficulty in building friendships and romantic relationships. In session one day, the hacker tells the therapist that he was easily able to obtain a great deal of personal information about her, including her home address, bank account balances, and social security number. He sees that the LMFT is unsettled by this, and assures her he has no intention of misusing the information. The LMFT should:

   a. **Incorrect.** Contact law enforcement and report the data theft, without revealing that the person suspected is a client. *It is not clear that the client has violated the law, and in order to say anything about the person suspected, the LMFT would have to reveal information learned in a confidential context.*

   b. **Incorrect.** Discontinue treatment and refer the client to at least three other therapists. *This could be considered client abandonment. While it may rightly be considered a boundary violation, given the nature of the treatment it would make more sense to address the issue clinically.*

   c. **Incorrect.** Make it a condition of treatment that the client delete all of this data from any place where he has it stored. *This would be a clinical consideration, not a legal or ethical issue for the therapist to address.*

   d. **CORRECT.** Consult with an attorney and monitor her accounts closely. *This is the appropriate response, though the LMFT would need to be cautious about what information is even shared with the attorney.*

69. A new client expresses surprise when she comes to her first session with an MFT and finds that the MFT's dog is resting next to the MFT's chair. The client expresses discomfort with the animal's presence, as the client was bitten by a dog when she was a child. Legally, the MFT should:

    a. **Incorrect.** Provide the client with a letter establishing that the dog is an Emotional Support Animal

    b. **Incorrect.** Diagnose the client's phobia as a disability and remove the dog from the room immediately

    c. **Incorrect.** Challenge the client's cognitive distortions, and use the opportunity to provide safe exposure to a well-controlled animal

    d. **CORRECT.** Provide information on the MFT's fee structure prior to beginning treatment

I hope you were quick to dismiss option (C) – challenging cognitive distortions is a clinical intervention, never a legal or ethical requirement. The federal regulations surrounding ESAs do not provide legal protection for an ESA within a therapist's office (A); an ESA letter has no benefit here. Option (B) gets out ahead of the situation described; we know that the client is experiencing discomfort, but that does not necessarily equate to a phobia or a disability. (Whether specific phobia qualifies as a disability is an interesting question in its own right, but it's not one that needs to be answered to rule out this response option.) It may seem a bit tangential, but this is a new client, and the MFT has a legal obligation to inform new clients of the fee structure prior to commencing treatment. Only option (D) addresses a legal responsibility for the MFT in the situation described.

70. A few days after a particularly difficult session, a client asks her therapist (an LMFT) to show her the information the LMFT wrote in the client's file about that session. The client had discussed childhood trauma and tells the LMFT she wants any information about that trauma removed immediately from the file. The LMFT empathizes with the client, but had included information about the trauma in progress notes and believes it is important to the client's treatment. Legally, the LMFT should:

    a. **Incorrect.** Comply with the client's request by sharing the progress note and removing any offending information from the file within 15 days.

    b. **CORRECT.** Inform the client that the client is free to review the file but that the LMFT cannot comply with the client's request to change the file. *It is the therapist, not the client, who determines the content of the file and must ensure it meets the standard of care. If the information about trauma is important to the treatment, it belongs in the file.*

    c. **Incorrect.** Inform the client that she may replace the progress note from the session with a statement of up to 250 words that she has written herself. *The client may add a statement to the file, but not to replace the therapist's existing record.*

    d. **Incorrect.** Refuse the client's request and process her reasons for wanting to keep the information secret. *The MFT cannot simply refuse to show the client the file. If the MFT believes that seeing the file will be harmful to the client, they must document that decision and inform the client that they can bring in another MFT of their choosing to review the file.*

71. A couple has been seeing an LMFT for premarital counseling. Toward the end of the counseling, they ask the LMFT whether she would be willing to attend the wedding and speak briefly at the reception about what makes the couple such a good fit. They say they have no problem with introducing the LMFT honestly and describing her role, saying she has been very help-ful to them. They believe their families would be happy to meet her and to share their thanks as well. The LMFT should:

   a. **Incorrect.** Politely refuse the request.
   b. **CORRECT.** Consider the cultural implications of the request and the potential impact on any future treatment.
   c. **Incorrect.** Attend the wedding, but decline to speak, and ask that she not be introduced as a therapist.
   d. **Incorrect.** Have the clients sign a release of information authorizing the LMFT to speak candidly, and then do so, consistent with the clients' request.

Accepting the invitation would arguably create a dual relationship. However, many such relationships are not prohibited. For a dual relationship that is not prohibited, therapists are required to consider the risk of exploitation for the client, and the impact on clinical judgment for the therapist. In this case, there is not enough information in the question to conclude that attending would be appropriate or inappropriate (options A or D). Asking to be falsely introduced (option C) may protect the clients' confidentiality but appears to go against why the clients want the therapist there. The LMFT should en-gage in the consideration spelled out in option B.

72. An adolescent male client tells an LMFT that he is drawn to violent movies and video games, and spends a great deal of time fantasizing about what he would do if confronted with a situation where he would need to become violent to survive. Though he has no history of violence or substance use, the client is struggling in school and the family has guns in the home. The LMFT should:

    a. **Incorrect.** Assess for safety and for psychotic disorder. *For an adolescent male to be drawn to violent movies and games is not particularly unusual, and is not evidence of a psychotic disorder.*

    b. **Incorrect.** Assess for substance use disorder. *No evidence of substance use disorder appears in the question.*

    c. **Incorrect.** Develop a safety plan. *The potentially violent fantasies and the presence of guns in the home are risk factors, but nothing in the question suggests an immediate safety concern.*

    d. **CORRECT.** Engage in discussion of what makes the games, movies, and fantasies so appealing. *No specific ethical or legal responsibilities are triggered by the information in the question.*

73. An Associate MFT has been working under supervision in a private practice setting for two years. The Associate achieves licensure, and informs the supervisor that the Associate will be starting their own private practice. The now-former Associate would like to bring their current clients along to the new practice. How can the Associate MFT best address their ethical responsibilities?

    a. **CORRECT.** Understand that the clients are ultimately clients of the supervisor, and allow the clients to determine how they wish to proceed.

    b. **Incorrect.** Understand that the clients are ultimately clients of the supervisor, and allow the supervisor to determine which clients may follow the new licensee into their private practice.

    c. **Incorrect.** Retain the files for all clients who wish to follow the new licensee into their private practice, allowing the supervisor to make copies if the supervisor wishes.

    d. **Incorrect.** Allow the clients to determine whether to follow the new licensee into private practice, paying the supervisor a fee for each client who does so. This fee covers the supervisor's costs for marketing that brought the clients in to see the Associate originally.

While supervisors bear ultimate responsibility for client well-being, clients retain their freedom of choice when it comes to selecting their treatment provider. The supervisor cannot make that choice for them (B). Files are the property of the employer, not the clinician seeing the client (C); clients following the new licensee to private practice would actually need to sign releases allowing the new licensee to copy current files and bring them along to the new practice. And paying a fee for referrals is explicitly prohibited by both ethical code and state law (D).

74. Your client has health insurance, but the insurance carrier is refusing to cover the client's therapy because she is seeing you for couple therapy and does not, in your assessment, qualify for a diagnosis of mental illness. You should:

    a. **Incorrect.** Assess the client's ability to advocate on her own behalf with the insurance company.
    b. **Incorrect.** Offer to include an "insurance diagnosis" on the client's paperwork to facilitate coverage.
    c. **CORRECT.** Work with the client to develop an alternative plan for payment.
    d. **Incorrect.** Discontinue therapy.

It is legal and fairly common for insurers to provide coverage for therapy only in the presence of a diagnosed mental illness. As such, you will need to work with the client on an alternative plan for payment. A is incorrect because the client's ability to advocate is not relevant; the insurance carrier is within the rules to refuse coverage. B is incorrect as the creation of a diagnosis solely for the purposes of insurance coverage, when the therapist does not believe the client actually qualifies for the diagnosis, would likely be considered insurance fraud. D is incorrect because a sudden discontinuation of therapy could be considered abandonment. While termination due to unpaid fees is ethically acceptable, in this case the client may be able to simply pay out of pocket. Choosing to discontinue therapy would be premature.

75. After consulting with an attorney and a colleague, an LMFT makes a child abuse report. The LMFT had learned from a family being seen together in treatment that the parents engage in physical punishment of their children. Three weeks after the report was made, the parents in the family ask directly in session whether the LMFT was the person who made the report. The parents have been frustrated and hope to confront the reporting party, as they do not believe their behavior is abusive and are embarrassed and angry that an investigator from the local child protective service agency visited their home and their child's school. The investigator was ultimately unable to substantiate the abuse report. Ethically, the LMFT should:

a. **CORRECT.** Acknowledge having made the report and share the specific reasons why the LMFT did so. *This is most in keeping with the general ethical principle of Fidelity.*

b. **Incorrect.** Acknowledge having made the report, apologize for having done so, and work to repair the relationship. *Presuming that the MFT had justifiable grounds for reporting, it would not be appropriate to apologize for having made the report.*

c. **Incorrect.** Deny having made the report, and empathize with their emotional response to the investigation. *Denying having made the report serves no clear ethical or legal purpose. It runs contrary to the general ethical principle of Fidelity.*

d. **Incorrect.** Deny having made the report, and guide the conversation back to the reasons why the family is in treatment. *Denying having made the report serves no clear ethical or legal purpose. It runs contrary to the general ethical principle of Fidelity.*

Appendix:
Exam Plan with Index

Board of Behavioral Sciences

Licensed Marriage and Family Therapist
California Law and Ethics Examination Outline

This document provides detailed information about the LMFT California Law and Ethics Examination, including a description of each content area, subarea and the associated task and knowledge statements.

Each question in the examination is linked to this content.

Note: The exam outline, including all task and knowledge statements, comes from the BBS outline published online. Page numbers in the following charts refer to where the relevant information can be found within this text.

I. Law (40%)

This area assesses the candidate's ability to identify and apply legal mandates to clinical practice.

IA. Confidentiality, Privilege, and Consent (14%)

Task Statement	Knowledge Statement	Page
T1. Comply with legal requirements regarding the maintenance/dissemination of confidential information to protect client's privacy.	K1. Knowledge of laws regarding confidential communications within the therapeutic relationship.	37
	K2. Knowledge of laws regarding the disclosure of confidential information to other individuals, professionals, agencies, or authorities.	37
T2. Identify holder of privilege by evaluating client's age, legal status, and/or content of therapy to determine requirements for providing treatment.	K3. Knowledge of laws regarding holder of privilege.	38
	K4. Knowledge of laws regarding privileged communication.	38
T3. Comply with legal requirements regarding the disclosure of privileged information to protect client's privacy in judicial/legal matters.	K4. Knowledge of laws regarding privileged communication.	38
	K5. Knowledge of laws regarding the release of privileged information.	39
	K6. Knowledge of legal requirements for responding to subpoenas and court orders.	39

Task Statement	Knowledge Statement	Page
T4. Comply with legal requirements regarding providing treatment to minor clients.	K1. Knowledge of laws regarding confidential communications within the therapeutic relationship.	37
	K2. Knowledge of laws regarding the disclosure of confidential information to other individuals, professionals, agencies, or authorities.	37
	K3. Knowledge of laws regarding holder of privilege.	38
	K4. Knowledge of laws regarding privileged communication.	38
	K7. Knowledge of legal criteria and requirements for providing treatment to minors.	40
T5. Maintain client records by adhering to legal requirements regarding documentation, storage, and disposal to protect the client's privacy and/or the therapeutic process.	K8. Knowledge of laws regarding documentation of therapeutic services.	40
	K9. Knowledge of laws pertaining to the maintenance/disposal of client records.	41
T6. Respond to requests for records by adhering to applicable laws and regulations to protect client's rights and/or safety.	K10. Knowledge of laws pertaining to client's access to treatment records.	41
	K11. Knowledge of laws pertaining to the release of client records to other individuals, professionals, or third parties.	41
T7. Provide services via information and communication technologies by complying with "telehealth" regulations.	K12. Knowledge of laws regarding the consent to and delivery of services via information and communication technologies.	42
T8. Comply with the Health Information Portability and Accountability Act (HIPAA) regulations as mandated by law.	K13. Knowledge of legal requirements of the Health Information Portability and Accountability Act (HIPAA).	43

IB. Limits to Confidentiality / Mandated Reporting (16%)

Task Statement	Knowledge Statement	Page
T9. Report known or suspected abuse, neglect, or exploitation of dependent adult client to protective authorities.	K14. Knowledge of indicators of abuse, neglect, or exploitation of dependent adults.	53
	K15. Knowledge of laws pertaining to the reporting of known or suspected incidents of abuse, neglect, or exploitation of dependent adults.	51
T10. Report known or suspected abuse, neglect, or exploitation of elderly client to protective authorities.	K16. Knowledge of indicators of abuse, neglect, or exploitation of elderly clients.	53
	K17. Knowledge of laws pertaining to the reporting of known or suspected incidents of abuse, neglect, or exploitation of elderly clients.	51
T11. Report known or suspected abuse or neglect of a child or adolescent to protective authorities.	K18. Knowledge of indicators of abuse/neglect of children and adolescents.	48
	K19. Knowledge of laws pertaining to the reporting of known or suspected incidents of abuse/neglect of children and adolescents.	48
T12. Comply with legal requirements regarding breaking confidentiality to protect the client in the presence of indictors of danger to self/others and/or grave disability.	K20. Knowledge of symptoms of mental impairment that may indicate the need for involuntary hospitalization.	54
	K21. Knowledge of legal requirements for initiating involuntary hospitalization.	55
	K22. Knowledge of laws regarding confidentiality in situations of client danger to self or others.	55

Task Statement	Knowledge Statement	Page
T13. Comply with legal requirements to report and protect when client expresses intent to cause harm to people or property.	K23. Knowledge of methods/criteria to identify situations in which client poses a danger to others.	56
	K24. Knowledge of laws pertaining to duty to protect when client indicates intent to cause harm.	57
	K25. Knowledge of situations/conditions that constitute reasonable indicators of client's intent to cause harm.	57
T14. Comply with legal requirements regarding privilege exceptions in client litigation or in response to breach of duty accusations.	K26. Knowledge of laws regarding privilege exceptions in litigation involving client's mental or emotional condition as raised by the client or client's representative.	58
	K27. Knowledge of laws regarding privilege exceptions in which client alleges breach of duty.	58
T15. Comply with legal requirements regarding privilege exceptions in court-appointed and/or defendant-requested evaluation/ therapy.	K28. Knowledge of laws regarding privilege exceptions in court-appointed evaluation or therapy.	58
	K29. Knowledge of laws pertaining to privilege exceptions in defendant-requested evaluation or therapy.	58
T16. Comply with legal requirements regarding reporting instances of crime perpetrated against minor clients.	K30. Knowledge of laws pertaining to the reporting of crimes perpetrated against a minor.	58
	K31. Knowledge of laws regarding privilege exceptions in crime or tort involving minors.	58

IC. Legal Standards for Professional Practice (10%)

Task Statement	Knowledge Statement	Page
T17. Comply with laws regarding sexual contact, conduct, and relations between therapist and client to prevent harm to the client and/or the therapeutic relationship.	K32. Knowledge of laws regarding sexual conduct between therapist and client.	62
	K33. Knowledge of legal requirements for providing client with the brochure *Therapy Never Includes Sexual Behavior.*	62
T18. Comply with legal parameters re: scope of practice.	K34. Knowledge of laws that define the scope of clinical practice.	63
T19. Comply with legal parameters regarding professional conduct.	K35. Knowledge of laws that define professional conduct for licensed practitioners.	63
T20. Disclose fee structure prior to initiating therapy.	K36. Knowledge of laws regarding disclosures required prior to initiating treatment.	66
T21. Comply with legal regulations regarding providing treatment when interacting with third-party payers.	K37. Knowledge of laws and regulations regarding third-party reimbursement.	66
	K38. Knowledge of parity laws regarding the provision of mental health services.	66
T22. Comply with laws regarding advertisement of services and professional qualifications.	K39. Knowledge of laws regarding advertisement and dissemination of information regarding professional qualifications, education, and professional affiliations.	67
T23. Comply with laws pertaining to the payment or acceptance of money or other consideration for referrals.	K40. Knowledge of legal requirements regarding payment or acceptance of money or other considerations for referral of services.	68

II. Ethics (60%)

This area assesses the candidate's ability to identify and apply ethical standards for professional conduct.

IIA. Professional Competence and Preventing Harm (18%)

Task Statement	Knowledge Statement	Page
T24. Consult with other professionals and/or seek additional education, training, and/or supervision to address therapeutic issues that arise outside the therapist's scope of competence.	K41. Knowledge of limitations of professional experience, education, and training to determine issues outside scope of competence.	74
	K42. Knowledge of situations that indicate a need for consultation with colleagues or other professionals.	74
	K43. Knowledge of ethical standards regarding the protection of client rights when engaging in consultation/collaboration with other professionals.	74
	K44. Knowledge of ethical methods of developing additional areas of practice or expanding competence.	75
	K45. Knowledge of the ethical responsibility to remain current in developments in the profession.	75
T25. Consult with other professionals to address questions regarding ethical obligations or practice responsibilities that arise during therapy.	K42. Knowledge of situations that indicate a need for consultation with colleagues or other professionals.	74
	K43. Knowledge of ethical standards regarding the protection of client rights when engaging in consultation/collaboration with other professionals.	74

Task Statement	Knowledge Statement	Page
T26. Evaluate therapist's own mental, emotional, or physical problems/impairments to determine impact on ability to provide competent therapeutic services.	K42. Knowledge of situations that indicate a need for consultation with colleagues or other professionals.	74
	K46. Knowledge of problems/impairments that interfere with the process of providing therapeutic services.	75
	K47. Knowledge of referrals and resources to assist in meeting the needs of clients.	76
	K48. Knowledge of methods to facilitate transfer when referrals to other professionals are made.	77
T27. Provide referrals to qualified professionals when adjunctive/alternate treatment would benefit the client.	K41. Knowledge of limitations of professional experience, education, and training to determine issues outside scope of competence.	74
	K43. Knowledge of ethical standards regarding the protection of client rights when engaging in consultation/collaboration with other professionals.	74
	K47. Knowledge of referrals and resources to assist in meeting the needs of clients.	76
	K48. Knowledge of methods to facilitate transfer when referrals to other professionals are made.	77
T28. Manage therapist's personal values, attitudes, and/or beliefs to prevent interference with effective provision of therapeutic services and/or the therapeutic relationship.	K49. Knowledge of the potential impact of therapist's personal values, attitudes, and/or beliefs on the therapeutic relationship.	76
	K50. Knowledge of methods for managing the impact of therapist's personal values, attitudes, and/or beliefs on the client or the therapeutic relationship.	77

Task Statement	Knowledge Statement	Page
T29. Evaluate potential conflict of interest situations to determine the impact on the client or the therapeutic process.	K51. Knowledge of conditions/situations that may impair judgment and/or lead to client exploitation.	77
	K52. Knowledge of methods for managing boundaries and/or professional relationships with the client.	78
	K53. Knowledge of methods for protecting the client and the therapeutic relationship in potential conflict of interest situations.	78
T30. Maintain professional boundaries with client to prevent situations or relationships that may impair professional judgment and/or adversely impact the therapeutic relationship.	K51. Knowledge of conditions/situations that may impair judgment and/or lead to client exploitation.	77
	K52. Knowledge of methods for managing boundaries and/or professional relationships with the client.	78
	K54. Knowledge of relationships that can be potentially detrimental to the client and/or the therapeutic relationship.	79
	K55. Knowledge of methods to prevent impairment to professional judgment and/or client exploitation in situations where dual/multiple relationships are unavoidable.	79
T31. Adhere to ethical guidelines regarding sexual intimacy/contact with prospective, current, or former clients and/or client's spouse, significant other, or family members to avoid causing harm or exploitation of the client.	K56. Knowledge of the potential for client harm or exploitation associated with sexual intimacy/contact between a client and therapist.	80
	K57. Knowledge of ethical standards pertaining to sexual intimacy/contact with clients and/or client's spouse, significant other, or family members.	81
	K58. Knowledge of ethical standards regarding entering into a therapeutic relationship with former sexual partners.	81

IIB. Therapeutic Relationship (27%)

Task Statement	Knowledge Statement	Page
T32. Obtain informed consent by providing client with information regarding the therapist and the treatment process to facilitate client's ability to make decisions.	K59. Knowledge of the ethical responsibility to provide client with information regarding the therapeutic process.	86
	K60. Knowledge of disclosures that facilitate client's ability to make decisions regarding treatment.	86
	K61. Knowledge of client's right to autonomy and to make decisions regarding treatment.	86
	K62. Knowledge of methods for communicating information pertaining to informed consent in a manner consistent with developmental and cultural factors.	87
	K63. Knowledge of the right and responsibility of legal guardian/representative to make decisions on behalf of clients unable to make informed decisions.	87
	K64. Knowledge of methods for protecting client's welfare when client is unable to provide voluntary consent.	87
T33. Evaluate for concurrent psychotherapy the client is receiving with other therapist(s) to determine implications for entering into a new therapeutic relationship.	K65. Knowledge of the effects of concurrent treatment relationships on the treatment process.	88
	K66. Knowledge of ethical guidelines for providing concurrent psychotherapy.	89
	K43. Knowledge of ethical standards regarding the protection of client rights when engaging in consultation/collaboration with other professionals.	74

Task Statement	Knowledge Statement	Page
T34. Address confidentiality and/or therapeutic issues associated with therapist's role, treatment modality, and/or involvement of third parties to protect the client's welfare and/or the therapeutic relationship.	K67. Knowledge of methods to identify the "client" and the nature of relationships when providing therapy to more than one person.	89
	K68. Knowledge of the impact of treatment unit, treatment modality, and/or involvement of multiple systems on confidentiality.	89
	K69. Knowledge of methods to manage factors that impact the therapeutic relationship.	90
	K70. Knowledge of methods to manage potential conflicts when providing concurrent therapy to more than one person.	91
	K71. Knowledge of methods for managing confidentiality and privacy issues when providing treatment to more than one person.	91
	K72. Knowledge of methods for managing confidentiality and privacy issues when treatment involves multiple systems or third parties.	91
T35. Manage the impact of confidentiality/limits of confidentiality on the therapeutic relationship by discussing with the client issues/implications that arise during the therapeutic process.	K73. Knowledge of ethical standards regarding the management of confidentiality issues that arise in the therapeutic process.	91
	K74. Knowledge of methods for managing the impact of confidentiality issues on the therapeutic relationship.	92
T36. Manage the impact of safety and/or crisis situations by evaluating risk factors to protect the client/others.	K75. Knowledge of methods for assessing level of potential danger or harm to client or others.	92
	K76. Knowledge of ethical obligations regarding the management of safety needs.	93
	K77. Knowledge of procedures for managing safety needs.	94

Task Statement	Knowledge Statement	Page
T37. Manage the impact of legal and ethical obligations that arise during the therapeutic process to protect the client/therapist relationship.	K78. Knowledge of the impact of legal and ethical obligations on the therapeutic relationship.	95
	K79. Knowledge of methods for protecting the best interest of the client in situations where legal and ethical obligations conflict.	96
	K80. Knowledge of methods for protecting the best interest of the client in situations where agency and ethical obligations conflict.	96
T38. Manage diversity factors in the therapeutic relationship by applying and/or gaining knowledge and awareness necessary to provide treatment sensitive to client needs.	K81. Knowledge of diversity factors that potentially impact the therapeutic process.	97
	K82. Knowledge of ethical standards regarding nondiscrimination.	96
	K83. Knowledge of ethical standards for providing services congruent with client diversity.	97
	K84. Knowledge of methods to gain knowledge, awareness, sensitivity, and skills necessary for working with clients from diverse populations.	97
T39. Provide treatment that respects client's autonomy and right to make decisions.	K85. Knowledge of the collaborative role between therapist and client in the therapeutic process.	98
	K61. Knowledge of client's right to autonomy and to make decisions regarding treatment.	86
	K86. Knowledge of methods to assist client make decisions and understand consequences.	98

Appendix: Exam Plan with Index

Task Statement	Knowledge Statement	Page
T40. Advocate with and/or on behalf of the client with third party payers to assist client in accessing mental health care.	K87. Knowledge of methods for evaluating client's capacity to advocate on own behalf.	99
	K88. Knowledge of ethical standards pertaining to interacting with third-party payers.	99
T41. Maintain practice procedures that provide for consistent care in the event therapy must be interrupted or discontinued.	K89. Knowledge of ethical considerations and conditions for interrupting or terminating therapy.	99
	K90. Knowledge of referrals/resources to provide consistent care in the event therapy must be interrupted or discontinued.	100
	K48. Knowledge of methods to facilitate transfer when referrals to other professionals are made.	77
T42. Terminate therapy when no longer required or no longer benefits the client.	K91. Knowledge of factors and/or conditions that indicate client is ready for termination of therapy.	101
	K92. Knowledge of factors and/or conditions that indicate client is not benefiting from treatment.	101
	K93. Knowledge of methods for managing the termination process.	101
	K94. Knowledge of methods to prevent client abandonment and/or client neglect.	101

297

IIC. Business Practices and Policies (15%)

Task Statement	Knowledge Statement	Page
T43. Advertise services by adhering to ethical guidelines regarding the use of accurate representations and information to promote services and/or expand practice.	K95. Knowledge of ethical guidelines regarding the use of accurate representation of qualifications and credentials in advertisements and/or solicitation of clients.	106
	K96. Knowledge of ethical guidelines pertaining to the solicitation of testimonials or statements from clients or others.	106
	K97. Knowledge of ethical guidelines regarding the recruitment of clients through employment and/or professional affiliations.	107
T44. Maintain client records by adhering to ethical guidelines to document treatment and/or protect the client's confidentiality.	K98. Knowledge of ethical guidelines regarding the documentation of therapeutic services consistent with clinical practice.	107
	K99. Knowledge of methods for providing reasonable protection of the confidentiality of client records.	108
	K100. Knowledge of ethical guidelines for releasing client records upon request.	108
T45. Clarify role(s) when acting in a professional capacity other than providing treatment or supervision to avoid confusion, maintain objectivity, and/or protect the therapeutic relationship.	K101. Knowledge of the ethical responsibility to clarify roles when acting in a professional capacity other than providing treatment or supervision.	108
	K102. Knowledge of ethical guidelines regarding engaging in conflicting and/or dual roles.	109
	K103. Knowledge of methods for maintaining impartiality and/or professional integrity when engaging in legal proceedings.	109

Task Statement	Knowledge Statement	Page
T46. Implement policies/procedures that address ethical issues associated with the use of electronic media and technology in the course of providing therapy.	K104. Knowledge of the potential for harm to the client or therapeutic relationship with the use of electronic media in the therapeutic process.	111
	K105. Knowledge of ethical standards for interacting with clients via electronic media.	110
	K106. Knowledge of the limitations and risks associated with electronic means of service delivery.	110
T47. Maintain fee/payment policies that are commensurate with services provided and protect the therapeutic relationship.	K107. Knowledge of methods and conditions for determining fees commensurate with professional services.	111
	K108. Knowledge of prohibited business practices/forms of remuneration for making/accepting client referrals.	111
	K109. Knowledge of the potential for client exploitation or harm that may result from bartering/exchanges for services.	111
	K110. Knowledge of ethical standards pertaining to the collection of unpaid balances.	113
	K111. Knowledge of ethical obligations regarding providing for continuation of treatment to the client.	113
	K112. Knowledge of ethical guidelines regarding the provision of therapeutic services when interacting with third-party payers.	113
	K47. Knowledge of referrals and resources to assist in meeting the needs of clients.	76

Task Statement	Knowledge Statement	Page
T48. Adhere to ethical guidelines regarding the acceptance of gifts and/or tokens of appreciation from clients.	K113. Knowledge of conditions/situations that may impair the integrity or efficacy of the therapeutic process.	114
	K114. Knowledge of ethical standards regarding the acceptance of gifts from clients.	114
T49. Adhere to ethical guidelines for protecting the welfare and dignity of participants when conducting research related to the provision of therapeutic services.	K115. Knowledge of procedures to safeguard participants when conducting research projects.	115
	K116. Knowledge of disclosures required to inform participants of the nature and role of research projects.	115
	K117. Knowledge of client rights regarding participation in research projects.	115
	K118. Knowledge of methods for protecting client confidentiality and data when conducting research projects.	116
T50. Address unethical or incompetent conduct of colleague by taking action to promote the welfare and interests of clients.	K119. Knowledge of conditions/situations that may impair the integrity or efficacy of the therapeutic process.	116
	K120. Knowledge of guidelines for addressing unethical or incompetent conduct of colleagues.	116
T51. Adhere to ethical guidelines for engaging in the supervisor/ prelicensure practitioner relationship.	K121. Knowledge of ethical guidelines governing the supervisor/prelicensure practitioner relationship and responsibilities.	117